LINES IN PLEASANT PLACES

One Man's Adventures of Faith in the Living God

Ron Kingham

Stonehaven Press
Bangor, CA
2020

Scripture quotations taken from The Holy Bible, New International Version ® NIV ® Copyright © 1973, 1978, 1984, 2011 by Biblica, Inc.™ are used by permission. All rights reserved worldwide.

Scripture quotations taken from the New American Standard Bible ® (NASB), Copyright © 1960, 1962, 1963, 1968, 1971, 1972, 1973, 1975, 1977, 1995 by The Lockman Foundation are used by permission. www.Lockman.org.

You may contact the author through:
Stonehaven Press
1747 Robinson Mill Rd.
Bangor, CA 95914

ISBN: 978-0-9898999-8-7

Dedication

There is a divine goodness in the plan of God regarding the transmission of life's wisdom from one generation to the next, and the keystone in that plan is the role a father plays in the development of his son. This book is about my development from childhood into manhood, and subsequently into man-of-God-hood, and it is gratefully dedicated to the memory of my amazing dad, Edward Kingham. He began investing in me from the moment of my birth, and long after his passing, his investments are still producing rich dividends.

Dad's life was a rich symbiosis of the love of life and the love of Jesus beautifully intertwined. He left a powerful impression on all the people he touched, but none is more deep and lasting than the imprint he left upon me. He was my template on how to overcome adversity and how to love excellence and craftsmanship. He taught and modeled resourcefulness and integrity. He showed me how to love God's creation and how to work hard. He was my example of genuine faith and sweet affection for the Word of God. Dad was my hero and my cheerleader. He was my model when I became a dad to my sons and daughter. And I wept when he was no longer there to answer the phone when I wanted to share something with him.

This book is about God's persistent work on my character development, and my story would have been quite different if Dad's fingerprints weren't all over my life.

Acknowledgements

I am humbly and deeply grateful to Arlene Hendriks for her astute editing of this manuscript. Her insights, growing out of her decades of counseling, were invaluable. I am also indebted to Donna McCoy whose keen eye for excellence assured a professional document. Most of all, I cannot express the depth of love and appreciation to my wife Dixie for her guidance and support through the project of reliving, re-emoting these memories, and documenting them here. She cheered me on with joy and inspiration. She was *way* more than an editor!

Contents

Introduction

Imagine yourself sitting around a campfire listening to my stories. They're personal stories about my life, beginning at birth and finishing with me as a seventy-three-year old man, so you might call this an autobiography. But seventy-three years is a long time, and huge chunks are missing here. So, these stories are selected to highlight important themes which I greatly desire to tell. They're not so much stories about my life, as much as they are stories about what my life has been about. Every story is true, at least as best as I can remember it, given the proclivities of memory.

In one sense, every person and their story is unique. In another sense, every person and their story is the same. The stories you will read here are uniquely mine. But my prayer is that you will find important points of correspondence with your own story. What we all share are our divine potential and our human brokenness. My story weaves its way through a labyrinth of experiences with both.

I'm an ordinary man. But I have known an extraordinary God. I started out hearing about God through the experience of others. But there came a point when that secondhand knowledge became firsthand, and the hearsay became the direct voice and actions of a personal living God. When an ordinary man aligns with an extraordinary God, amazing things take place, not because of the man, but because of the divine enablement within the man. In these pages, you will read of some of the remarkable things God has done in and around my life, and as you do, please remember the first two sentences of this paragraph. When God dramatically intervened, I was as blessed in the moment as I pray you will be in the reading of it.

I recently read the autobiography of an exceedingly narcissistic man. At times I wanted to gag because it was all about his accomplishments and lecherous passions. Oh, how I pray that you do not have that experience as you read this book. To tell a first-person story, one must use the first person pronouns profusely. Please do not equate the presence of the pronouns with a desire to flaunt or inflate myself. My intended purpose is quite the opposite. I hunger to heap great praise upon the One who created and redeemed me by His precious blood.

Some of you may have been present for one or more of these stories. Remember that what you are reading here is how the story was witnessed through my eyes. I am sharing what was going on inside of me, and sometimes I didn't understand it fully at the moment. Now I'm writing from a more mature and retrospective vantage point. It has been an emotional ride for me to re-live these many adventures, and the people who have been so important at various stages of my life have paraded before me. Thank God for friends, family, and partners in ministry. I mention a lot of names in this book. Intentionally. The names are not changed. I want to acknowledge how these various people played a role in what God was doing in, through, and around me. My life has been touched by tens of hundreds of people, but the ones who appear in the lines of these stories played key roles in these particular stories.

So settle back with that campfire crackling in the background of your mind. Here's the story of my adventure of faith in an amazing God.

Ron Kingham
Bangor, CA
May 2020

1

Ronnie

My mother's elbow jabbed my father's rib as he lay sleeping beside her. "Ed! Wake up! The water broke!" she screamed. And then she watched in puzzled disbelief as Dad dutifully made his way to the closet, pulled on his work pants, shirt, and boots, and disappeared down the stairs into the basement.

Dad was about sixteen when his normal hearing began to slide precipitously into deafness. In the space of a just a few short months, the little bones in his inner ears inexplicably fused themselves together, and he became almost completely deaf. Quite a blow to an otherwise healthy, athletic and outgoing teenager who sang the lead role in the Palo Alto High School operetta and was an Eagle Scout. He had to learn to read lips and navigate young manhood in silence. It wasn't until his mid-twenties that he was able to acquire a crude hearing aid (about the size of a pack of cigarettes that hung from a pocket sling on his chest). He wore this until the day of his death. He told me years later how he wept as he heard the nearly forgotten song of birds out the window of the audiologist's office. Accordingly, all my memories of Dad were colored by his hearing loss. My sister, Judy, and I instinctively learned to check for the presence of the huge ear piece with a cord running down his neck whenever we wanted to talk with him.

If it wasn't there, we had to scream into his "good" ear or use sign language. To this day, I am still in awe of the way Dad overcame that serious handicap and lived his life to the fullest without complaint. Many people never knew of his hearing loss. But Mom certainly did.

So since Dad was almost stone deaf at night without his hearing aid, Mom had made sure he had heard her announcement that she was in serious labor. He was able to hear "water"—and sensing Mom's urgency, he had assumed that the problem was serious. So after about five minutes in the basement of their apartment in Oakland, Dad reappeared to see my mom in a panic. "I can't find any pipes leaking," he said, puzzled. "What are you talking about?"

Mom pointed to her belly and screamed, "*My* water broke!"

It was September 21, 1946, the day I made my appearance into this world in Oakland, California, the firstborn of Edward and Inez Kingham. That makes me one of the original baby boomers, having begun my earthly sojourn when I was conceived just four months after the end of World War II.

I heard my mom regale countless friends and guests through the years with the hilarious story of Dad in his boots trying to fix the water that broke. It became a legend in our family.

Dad's hearing loss had rendered him 4F for the draft, so he served as a civilian during the war in the carpenter shop at Mare Island Naval Shipyard on the northern edge of San Francisco Bay. He grew up in a family of builders and had taken to carpentry with extraordinary skill. It is very likely he performed carpentry repairs on the U.S.S. Indianapolis while it was at Mare Island to be patched up after damaging engagements in the Pacific Theater. It was the cruiser that transported the atomic bomb the American forces dropped on Hiroshima, Japan.

After the war, Dad found himself looking for carpentry work wherever he could find it. But he was an entrepreneur at heart, so shortly after I was born, he ventured out into the wilds of largely undeveloped Santa Cruz County, California, with a vision of starting his own business as a building contractor and property developer. He studied and secured his contractor's license and hung out his shingle with his brother Bob: "Kingham Brothers Contractors." With the help of a loan from his father-in-law Henry Cerrina, he bought acreage in the raw, undeveloped redwood forest above Ben Lomand.

There he built my first family home. It was a tiny rustic single-wall cabin framed from native redwood. It had running water—a tank on the roof which was filled by buckets drawn from a nearby spring. Dad would drive to the spring, fill the containers and then drive up to the cabin and stand on top of the car to fill the tank. It was a rainy winter that first year, and my dear mother was miserable. The redwood forest is magnificent... but the trees are tall, and it's dark in the middle of the day in winter. She was used to the connected urban life of her Italian community in 1940s Oakland. Now she was caring for a one-year-old in isolation, far from civilization.

I was too young to have any memories of life in the Ben Lomand cabin. But there is one story which emerges from those days that introduces the theme I want to begin unfolding in this memoir. My life truly has been an echo of Psalm 16:6: "The boundary lines have fallen for me in pleasant places; surely I have a delightful inheritance" (NIV). A huge piece of my inheritance is the home God chose to place me in. I have known a *lot* of people over my lifetime; in my pastoral ministry

I have probed into the familial history of scores of people; and I have observed thousands of people in the world around us. So often the thorny difficulties which plague our world find their roots in parents who haven't dealt with their own "stuff" and create an atmosphere in the home which is not conducive to healthy child development. I believe the scriptures teach that God, in His wise and gracious sovereignty, creates each child with a purpose and places them with the parents whom He desires (see e.g. Jeremiah 1:5, Galatians 1:15). We don't get to choose our parents. God does that for us. For those whom He places in difficult homes, He has plans to rescue them and give them a life-message which will exalt the grace of God. For those whom He places with emotionally healthy, Christ-honoring parents, He expects a good return on His investment. In my case, He lavished undeserved goodness upon me. I have often felt embarrassed when other folks tell their stories of parents who were drug addicts or alcoholics or angry atheists or philanderers—or worse. Such was not my story. And as you will see unfolding in this book, all of my adult life I have felt a compelling drive to return the blessing on those around me. Jesus said that from whom much is given, much is required. To this present moment, I take that seriously.

My parents each had a personal encounter with God at a young age. They were both reared in the fellowship of the Plymouth Brethren meetings which were flourishing in their youth in the Bay Area. Both made public professions of their faith in Jesus in the PB meetings (Mom in the Oakland Meeting and Dad in the Palo Alto Meeting). Mom's faith in Jesus was very simple. It shaped her values and caused her to work in beautiful harmony with Dad as the obvious leader of our home. Dad's faith was deep and inquisitive. He read widely, studied deeply, and lived what he believed. He became a counselor to many and taught classes at church. He conducted his business with scrupulous integrity, and he had an abiding relationship with Jesus which fashioned everything he did. His was not a Sunday religion.

Two kinds of construction were going on in Ben Lomand back in 1948: Dad's young Christian manhood was still under construction in his heart while his hands were building the Ben Lomand cabin. Jesus was lovingly adding His righteous character into him while at the same time burning away various inappropriate attitudes and behaviors which were still hanging around. At some time in his twenties—I think motivated by the iconic model of Winston Churchill—he had picked up smoking an occasional cigar while he worked. I was close to two years old. Mom bundled me up and put me in a safe place to watch daddy work. He was puffing away on a stogie. He told me later He had been under the conviction of the Holy Spirit for a while that smoking was not good for his life and testimony—especially as a singer (Dad, despite his hearing handicap, had an opera quality voice). But he enjoyed his cigars. Next thing you know, I found a stick roughly the size and shape of a cigar and started "smoking" it—as young boys are apt to do, imitating their fathers. That was the last cigar he smoked! He told me later that God's Spirit showed him his example to me was far more important than any enjoyment he might receive from smoking a silly cigar.

The cigar story became symbolic of the way he lived the rest of his days. He was always allowing the Spirit to shape his life to be the best possible man and husband and father. He was certainly flawed like the rest of us, but he knew how to appropriate the grace of God to shore up his weaknesses and intensify his strengths. I praise God for the godly influence of my parents. It became the backdrop to the rest of my life. And more than that, I thank God for the example they set. My parents are a huge part of what God used to shape me into the man I became. There was never any abuse—verbal or physical, never any fighting or yelling. And there was always an abundance of love and encouragement.

As I said, Mom was flirting with melancholy the whole time we were in the redwood cabin. So as Dad traveled about the county in his business, he found and purchased a lot in a new subdivision in Scotts Valley called Mañana Woods. There he built a simple little three-bedroom-one-bath, sold the cabin, and we began our life as a family in Scotts Valley/Santa Cruz. It was 1950 and I was four. We had a sprinkling of neighbors, but the neighborhood was sparsely populated with a lot of vacant lots for a boy to dig in the dirt, play sandlot baseball, ride a bike (and later a homemade go-kart), explore the nearby redwoods, and pick wild blackberries. We lived in that house for five years, the setting for my earliest memories as I toddled around in my knee pants with shoulder straps.

I think building and construction are in my genes. My great grandfather John Kingham was a builder in Palo Alto. His son Lionel Kingham was also a builder in Palo Alto. And of course, my dad, Edward Kingham, was a builder, contractor, and developer in Santa Cruz. My propensity to swinging a hammer showed up early. I remember finding a can of small nails and a hammer and deciding to help daddy with the brand new kitchen cabinets he had just built. I think Mom was outside hanging up the laundry while I quickly drove about twenty nails (didn't bend very many at all, thank you very much!) into the end of the cabinet. Of course, Daddy wasn't quite as pleased as I had hoped…. My posterior felt the pain, and I learned an early lesson about asking permission before I drove a nail. Dad set me up with my own hammer and a big block of wood for pounding my little heart out—and I played with it a lot.

Mom got pregnant with my sister Judy early in 1951, and she had a very difficult pregnancy. She was often sick. One of my earliest memories is of a day when she went running into the bathroom, and I watched as she threw up her breakfast. The sight, sound, and smell of vomit threw me into a fearful state. I ran into my room, slammed and locked the door, and sat there for a couple hours with my fingers in my ears. Mom needed my help, but I would not come out, no matter how sick she was. I stayed till I was sure the episode was over. I relate that incident because it provides context for the rest of my story. Throughout this book, I will be relating how I have grown, how I have faced serious deficiencies in my character—often displayed at moments of crisis—and have been changed by the grace of God. I believe God wisely tailors our experiences to expose our need for His transforming grace. For now, let me simply say that God has marvelously transformed my fear of vomit.

My wonderful little sister Judy was born in February 1952, and from that point forward I was part of a family of four. But Judy and I are five and half years apart, so we had little in common in our lives away from home. However at home, we got along marvelously well. I am hard pressed to remember any fight we ever had.

Scotts Valley School had no kindergarten in 1952, so my formal education began in the first grade. I rode the bus to school in the early years. But in later years I enjoyed the solitude of the mile-plus walk down the hill every day. School was never hard for me. God gave me an inquisitive mind and a fairly good memory. From my very young years it became apparent that my natural skills were academic—particularly math and science. I definitely was not an athlete. All the other boys could outrun me and outplay me on the ball field. I can still feel the pain at recess when the teacher would organize teams to play baseball. She would appoint the two best athletes as captains who would then choose their team mates. The rest of us would line up against the fence. I would invariably be the last person chosen. I remember trying out for the school basketball team: what a joke! I was the shortest kid in the group of hopefuls and was cut the first day of tryouts. I carried this blight of inferiority on my male ego all through my school years, and it wasn't until my last year of high school that I was finally able to "prove" my manhood athletically.

At home it was different. I was my mom's fair-haired son and my dad's little buddy. (I remained his little buddy all his days, as he was a lanky 6'4", and I achieved all of 5'7" in my adult height!) Mom was a happy homemaker. Her Italian heritage taught her to be a marvelous cook, so I acquired a slightly "chunky" shape and wore "relaxed fit" jeans. I figured out much later that part of Mom's self-esteem was embodied in the meals she presented to her family. If we didn't indulge fully—eat large quantities of her delicious presentations—she felt slighted. I can assure you that I did more than my share of affirming Mom's worth every day at the table! She taught me to do basic chores such as the dishes and yard work. I grew to love doing a nice neat job pulling weeds, mowing the lawn, and sweeping the driveway and walks.

Dad was thoroughly engaged with his new business which became known as Kingham Construction, and he was heavily involved with church—Twin Lakes Baptist Church (TLBC), a block from the beach in Santa Cruz. He sang often over the radio for the Sunday evening services, he served on leadership boards, and he taught classes. But he regularly found time for Judy and me. He took me out to his jobs whenever he could. It exposed me to the world of building. Sometimes we went fishing together. Sometimes it was throwing the football. But he always led us in family worship, usually around the breakfast table. He would read from the Bible; we would talk about what we had read; and he would lead us in a song and/or a prayer. It set the tone for a family who enjoyed life together and was dedicated to following Jesus.

I was six years old. It was Sunday after church. Baby Judy (six months old) was down for her nap. The three of us were seated around the kitchen table enjoying the wonderful Sunday dinner Mom had prepared. Dad often liked to tune the radio to the "Old Fashioned Revival Hour" with Charles Fuller and listen while we ate. For some reason (I know now that it was the presence of the Holy Spirit), I was riveted to the message he preached. As Dr. Fuller began to invite his listeners to receive Jesus, I began to feel the conviction of sin come over my little body. I realized I had a lot of sin, and I wanted Jesus to forgive me. So I told my daddy. He led me to my room where we knelt by the bed, and I invited Jesus into my life to forgive me and take me to heaven with Him when I died. Jesus entered my life at that moment, but He wasn't truly welcomed there yet.

Thus began an adventure of faith which has defined my path ever since. I wish, however, I could say my growth was steadily upwards from that moment by the radio in the house at 240 La Cuesta Drive, but it wasn't. For the next thirteen years I would describe myself simply as a good kid, a moral kid, a church kid, a kid who didn't live like the worldly kids, a kid whose parents were Christians, a kid who talked the talk without walking the walk. I didn't develop any kind of personal intimacy with God, and the seed of my faith was in danger of being snatched away by Satan. Praise God, that seed finally took root in my second year of college after a serious crisis of faith in which I came precariously close to pitching my "useless" faith.

At age nine, I saw others being baptized, and I wanted to be like them. It was what the good church kids did. So I was baptized in the tank behind the choir loft at Twin Lakes Baptist Church in the fall of 1955. But to illustrate the state of my spiritual life at that time, I was more enamored with the quick-change artistry of Pastor Kraft than Jesus Himself. Roy Kraft had streamlined a technique of rolling up his sleeves and slipping into a pair of high-waist fishing waders without removing his Sunday best. He could perform the baptism and be back on the stage by the third stanza of the hymn which followed the dunking. It was spectacular!

It's painful for me to admit it now, but for much of those thirteen years between 1952 and 1965, I was the hypocrite Jesus talked about when He quoted Isaiah, "This people draw near with their words and honor Me with their lip service, but they remove their hearts far from Me, and their reverence for Me consists of tradition learned by rote" (Isaiah 29:13, NASB). Of course, there were occasional moments, particularly at church summer camp's victory circle, when my faith would be revived, but then it would retract to its ambient dormancy. So as I relate the events of my childhood and teenage years, keep in mind that I had not fully entered into life as a bona fide follower of Christ.

One of the wonderful things about the way God graciously made me is that I learn well from my mistakes. This theme will weave its way throughout the remaining pages of this book. One of the early examples happened when I was about seven. I remember playing with one of Dad's tools -

without his permission and then not putting it back in its proper place. I clearly disobeyed his rules. When Mom figured this out, she told me she would report it to Dad when he got home from work. She did, and, as feared, Dad hustled me off to the familiar spot in my bedroom where he periodically "applied the board of education to my seat of learning." He talked with me about the errors of my ways and then lovingly, but firmly, whacked me on the backside. It hurt badly, and I cried for a while. An hour or so passed, and I decided to approach my dad with a question: "I don't like spankings! What do I have to do to avoid another spanking like that?"

Dad thought for a minute and said, "Well, just obey your mom and dad, and we'll never spank you again." Believe it or not, my posterior never got warmed and reddened again! I learned to obey and never looked back. From my present vantage point, I can see that this was a pivotal step in my later spiritual development. It taught me the joy of obeying my loving Heavenly Father at all times rather than disobeying Him and reaping the consequences.

In the fall of 1955, Dad completed construction on a new home at 341 La Cuesta Drive, just five doors down the street from our current home. It was a classy upgrade with more rooms, two-and-a-half baths, a three-car garage, and offices for Dad's business set on a hill with a view of Scotts Valley. It was my home until I headed off to college. It was the place I learned to play the piano, the trombone, the guitar, the Jew's harp, and the gut bucket. It was where I learned the joy of cutting, splitting and burning firewood. It was where I donned puberty and sprouted my first whiskers. It was where I learned to drive and where I parked my first car, a '58 Chevy Biscayne. It was the venue where I would bring a cute, perky young lady named Cathy Campbell to be introduced to my parents and my friends as my fiancée.

It was also the place where I learned God wired me as a morning person, which at times set me at odds with much of the rest of the world, including my Lord Jesus who regularly stayed awake all night in prayer. Being a morning person is a double-edged sword. The early bird truly does get the worm, but he also misses out on much social life. The early signs showed up when my parents enrolled me in the Bible Memory Association program. Each week I was assigned a chunk of scripture to memorize in the King James Version and then recite verbatim to my "hearer" to win a prize. I loved the rewards and the approbation, so I happily learned the verses. (Much of that scripture is still with me to this day, for which I praise God.) Somehow I figured out that the preeminent time of the day for me to do my memory work was the wee hours of the morning before anyone else in the house was awake. My brain was quick and active at 4:00 AM, but it would become sorrowfully dull and fuzzy in the evenings after dinner.

To this day, my primary study time is in the mornings, and I'm careful to avoid important decisions in the evening. This inability to function well in the evenings struck a serious blow to my social life with my friends and contemporaries who loved to party late into the night. This played out quite dramatically to me when I was a senior in high school. Our church youth group planned an all-night grad party after the ceremonies were over at the high school. They put us on a bus about 10:00 PM and started carting us around to fun places like a swimming pool, a skating rink, a bowling alley and a pizza parlor. The rest of the kids were bristling with enthusiasm, while I was either drowsy or completely zonked out in the back of the bus. It took me a couple days to recover from the hangover-like malaise of missing my sleep.

Stories about this incapacity of mine still circulate around Woodland from my years there. On more than one embarrassing occasion I fell asleep standing up in the kitchen while I was attempting to politely encourage evening guests it was time for them to find their way home! One time a friend caught me as I went down, saving me from cracking my head on the kitchen counter. On several occasions when my kids were in their late teens and staying out late with their friends, I met them coming in the door as I was going out the door for an early morning event or discipleship meeting.

This malady became particularly egregious to my sweet bride Cathy when we began our life together as husband and wife. In my enthusiastic optimism, I promised her we would kneel at the bed each night for prayer at the end of the day. The first night I got on my knees and started to pray. But by the third sentence I keeled over out cold. We figured out we were going to have to learn to pray within my hours of functionality! My kids will all remember times when I was reading them a bedtime story, and I would fall asleep in the middle of a sentence, slurring the last couple words as the lights went out. As they grew older, it was not uncommon for them all to be loudly playing games and making music in the living room while I snored close-by on the couch.

So a very wonderful part of my story is the way God has redeemed my evening weakness. He has used me despite the fact that I was often on an entirely different time schedule than most of the people around me. He has enabled me to take ownership of the circadian rhythms He sovereignly implanted within me. Everyone's journey into adulthood is fraught with much painful self-discovery. I praise God that He has transformed the lemons of my evening weakness into the sweet lemonade of much morning productivity. And I'm good with it, praise God!

At just about the same time we moved into the new home at 341 La Cuesta Dr., Dad also "happened" onto one of the most significant properties of his entire career as a real estate developer. It was one of those deals I learned about many years later that property investors call a sleeper. One of his friends from church, Lloyd Johnson, called and rather matter-of-factly asked, "Hey Ed, I'm going up to the tax sale in Mariposa County this week. Would you like to buy a lot in Yosemite?"

Lloyd was a notorious jokester, so Dad went along with the apparent prank and said, "Sure. I'll give you a hundred bucks." Well, long story short, it wasn't a prank. And both Dad and Lloyd bought side-by-side lots inside the park boundaries on a western plateau called Foresta. The lots were surrounded by park-owned land, so we couldn't see other cabins from our property. They acquired the grant deeds for the mere sum of the $100 tax due on each parcel. And from 1955 to 1990 the Kinghams and Johnsons enjoyed the unfathomable privileges of having a cabin in Yosemite. While the teeming multitudes were packed into the official park campgrounds, we had our spacious, quiet place to ourselves. It was a fairy tale come true. I had the fun of helping Dad and Lloyd build a tiny cabin on our lot in the summer of '56. I was only ten, so my help was pretty minimal, but the bonding time with Dad was golden.

When I was about twelve, Dad decided we needed to dig a well at the Yosemite property for our water. Up to that time, we had been hauling water from a creek or a spring. First, Dad located the well by dowsing, assuring us we should hit water at a fairly shallow level. Then Dad and Lloyd started a three-foot diameter hole and got it down as far as they could throw the dirt out with a shovel. About the time they quit, the earth had changed from top soil to decomposed granite, and the water was beginning to moisten the hole. Then they said, "OK, Ron, it's your turn. We need a little guy to go down in the hole (I was about 4'8" at that point.) and work with a digging bar and scoop buckets of the gravelly water-bearing earth, and we'll pull them up with a rope."

It was a warm summer day, and it was an absolute delight for me to be digging in the loose, damp gravel and going deeper and deeper. As I watched the bucket rise each time, the little circle of light got smaller and smaller. As I got into the stratum which was really flowing nicely with water, it became difficult to bail the water out as fast as it was coming in. So it was time to stop.

Then it dawned on me: I was about twenty feet down in the hole. How could I possibly get out? I have shared this story with many people in recent years, because it illustrates the role mentors and friends play in the lives of people who have gotten themselves into holes from which they can't extricate themselves—whether from tough experiences or poor choices.

As it turns out, Lloyd Johnson had been manning the bucket at the top, and—unbeknownst to me—Dad had been busying himself constructing a long ladder from redwood 2x2s left over from building the cabin. They lowered the long ladder down to me, and I easily ascended out of the pit. Dad affixed a hand-operated pitcher pump to the top of that well, and from that day onward, it provided us delicious water all the days of the cabin.

Yosemite looms large in my childhood memories: camping, hiking, swimming, fishing, sitting around the campfire playing my guitar, backpacking with my dad, scaling

Half Dome with my two oldest sons, telling bear stories, quietly communing with the Creator in one of earth's most spectacular displays of His majesty.... The list is endless. It was my favorite summer destination both during my days with my parents and then for the first twenty-one years of my own family.

Watching our cabin burn in the horrendous fire of 1990 was one of the most gut-wrenching disasters I have ever witnessed. My whole family and I were just arriving on the ridge above Foresta in two vehicles and a tent trailer teeming with gear and supplies for two weeks at the cabin when the fire erupted from a lightning strike in the Merced River canyon and roared its way towards the cabin. Seeing one-hundred-fifty-foot tall pine trees exploding with three-hundred-foot high flames like matches being struck by a mythical giant rendered me speechless. I remember finding my way to a pay phone to call Dad to let him know the cabin was burning, and I literally was unable to talk. I'll mention more about that fire a little later.

I'm grateful to God that I was amazingly healthy throughout my childhood and teenage years. Of course, there were moments.... Nearly every winter (when the leaves are off the plants) I would contract a nasty case of poison oak which would put me down for about a week with eyes swollen shut and itchy red rashes all over my body, particularly in places which don't often see the sun. In high school I faced down my poison oak fear (at my dad's prompting) by drinking the actual oil extracted from poison oak. My immune system sweetly did what God created it to do, and from that time on, I have not been bothered by poison oak.

I broke my left arm twice (at ages six and fourteen), and I lost a quarter-sized chunk of my face to a rather horrific dog bite at age seven. I was playing with my next door

26

neighbor's dog. I innocently picked up his bone and started to hand it to him, and he lunged at my face. That trauma birthed a serious distaste for dogs within me which followed me for the rest of my days—at least until Ron 2.0 (which you will read about in Chapter 13)! One of the reasons I wear facial hair today is to camouflage the scar.

Then there was the duck hunting incident. I am reminded of it every time I receive X-rays at a new dentist's office. Dad bought into a twelve-member duck club in Los Banos. It had twelve concrete blinds carefully spaced out around the watery pond so the occupants couldn't shoot each other. Every time I went hunting with Dad, someone was missing that day, so I got to use their vacant blind. Every time except once, that is…. On that occasion every blind was occupied, so Dad took the blind close to a hole in the mud where a man in waders could stand, waist deep in the water. We took turns—one of us in the blind and one of us in the hole. We made a pact that since the hole was pretty close to the blind, we would not shoot in each other's direction. It was my turn in the blind. My head just protruded above the concrete lip of the blind. I heard dad begin to call a mallard. I watched with anticipation as the duck responded and began to move towards him. Dad lifted his shotgun and started to track with the descending fowl. It was a grey winter morning and it was easy to lose all sense of direction. Then I watched in horror as the duck started letting down for a landing right in between us. *"He won't shoot, will he?"* I thought in disbelief.

But he did! At the crack of Dad's gun, I instinctively jerked my head sideways as I felt the smack of five pellets penetrating the side of my face and neck (where they still reside). "You shot me!" I screamed, thinking I might be dying. (Dad did kill the duck!)

But actually I *wasn't* dying, and it didn't even hurt! Dad literally ran from "the hole" to my blind—quite a feat in two feet of water with eight inches of gooey mud at the bottom. He rushed me to the local clinic in Los Banos where the examining physician told us that since the pellets were stainless steel, it would be best to leave them. Then as the excitement faded and we began to analyze what had happened, we were in awe of God's protective grace: one of the pellets had missed my eye by one quarter inch; one missed my ear by one quarter inch. And none did any damage to the crucial array of nerves and blood vessels which lace the face and neck. I walked away literally unscathed. This was early evidence that God had His provident hand of protection upon me and had important things for me to do in the years to come. I saw God miraculously restore my hand about fourteen years later. I'll share that story in a subsequent chapter.

I had my first official "date" with a girl when I was in eighth grade. The leaders of our church youth group planned a special dinner for us kids in the spring of 1960. It was advertised as a fancy dress-up affair, and we were all supposed to pair off and bring a date. I did not want to be seen with *any* of the girls in my Junior High group. So I pleaded with my Mom to just stay home. But she had another idea: "How about you ask Linda Lewis, the girl you met when we visited with the Lewises last summer. They attend the Alliance Church. She's in your grade. You seemed to get along well with her when we were over at their house."

So I succumbed to her prodding. I called her on the phone. "Hi, this is Ronnie Kingham. Do you remember me from last summer? Would you like to go to our spring banquet with me?" Amazingly, she said yes.

The big night arrived, and I dressed up in my coat and tie. Dad drove me over to her place. Mom had instructed me to take a corsage with me. So I got out of the huge tan Mercury—all 4'11" of me, still not in puberty—and I walked up to her door, corsage in hand. She opened the door. The outside walk was about six inches below the house floor height which simply added six more inches of insult to the way I felt as I looked up at this almost-woman towering above me. She was probably about 5'8", and a very attractive young lady in the early bloom of her womanhood. In the nine months since we had seen each other she had been transformed, but I was still the little wimpy boy who did not belong in the same league with her. As we walked into the church together, my head was right at the height of the corsage I had given her, and I just wanted out of there. Linda was a perfect lady, but *I* could not wait for that long evening to be over with. It was a long time before I even considered another date!

That story of my first date sheds light on the intensity of the emotional struggle that churned within me during those pre-adolescent and adolescent years. I definitely felt inferior to my peers according to the values with which peers measure one another. My short stature, late hormonal development, and non-athleticism took a toll on my self-esteem. So in response, I excelled in the arenas where I could, particularly academics. I consistently did well in school, I think, partly because I learned how to listen, ask questions, and study, and partly because Dad was regularly challenging me, "Ron, think it through." However, my academic success must be evaluated in light of this caveat: I hated to read, and I did everything I could to avoid reading books. I remember counting the number of books I had read by the time I graduated from college. It was about twenty. One year while I was still in grammar school I was chatting with my neighbor, Elaine Weller, as we were walking home from the bus stop after school. School was about to dismiss for the summer, and we were talking about what we were going to do with the free time in the summer. I spoke about all kinds of projects and games and outdoor activities and work for my dad on his jobs, and she said she couldn't wait to begin sitting on her chaise lounge and reading a huge stack of novels all summer. I shook my head in bewilderment. The very thought of it made me shiver. As I look back, I rejoice in the way God has transformed this glaring weakness in me. Books have become an integral part of my life, and there never seems to be enough time to read what I want to read. But that's not the way I started.

The summer between eighth grade and my freshman year in high school, I made the announcement to my parents and friends that I would no longer be known as Ronnie. From that point on, everyone was to call me Ron. My peers were maturing around me, and I needed something to assure me I was also growing up. So while I was waxing my crewcut to stand up and forming my shrink-to-fit Levis around coffee cans, I started to swagger just a little in my newfound self-proclamation: "I am Ron, the high schooler." But, to be sure, the remnants of Ronnie continued to dog me onto the campus. Growing up is such a painful thing!

2

High School—from Wimp to BMOC

Santa Cruz was growing rapidly in the early 60s. So I attended two years at the old Santa Cruz High School campus and then finished out my junior and senior years at the brand new Soquel High School. I entered SCHS at 4'11" and still not in puberty, but by the time I reached Soquel, the hormones were flowing.

One of the ways I compensated for my height insecurity was to deepen my interest and involvment in music. My early foundation on the piano as well as my regular participation in church music stood me in good stead for later forays into musical endeavors, especially in college. I loved to sing the hymns, especially as my voice began to drop into the bass range. I enjoyed playing trombone for the SCHS marching band. We played for the football games and marched in parades down Pacific Avenue. But the trombone just wasn't "cool," so that lasted only one year. I became fascinated with folk music which was on the rise in those days, so Mom got me my first guitar. I taught myself basic chords—enough to lead sing-alongs at church and camp and Yosemite. Sadly, I never took a lesson, so I didn't learn how to pick. My lackluster ability with the guitar caused me to switch to the standup bass in college when I was exposed to real guitar players. Our church youth group loved to hold "sings." We would gather around the piano or the guitar and sing our little hearts out. I also sang with the church youth choir; we even toured on a bus.

For a brief season, a church friend, Dave Glass, and I banded together, labeling ourselves Dirty Dave and Rotten Ron. We performed at several special events. Dave had an uncanny ability to listen to musical groups on records and memorize every word of every song. So he was the main vocalist. I backed him up and played along on the Jew's harp and the gut bucket. We specialized in corny, humorous songs. Dave's mannerisms and shifty eyes added a great level of humor to the performances. Of course, my mom was quite proud that her son was a performer!

As I entered high school, I was becoming aware that I was naturally bent towards mechanical things, mathematical problem solving, science, etc. So the high school guidance counselor steered my courses toward pre-engineering. I was delighted, because in math and science you just solve problems and don't read books and write essays (both of which I disliked *very* much). I stayed on that path all the way through college. Looking back from my present vantage point, I marvel at the way God has used my mechanical skills all the way through my life. That will be evident in the coming chapters. But what is wonderful to me is the way God starting opening my mind and heart to love books and writing in the years after college. I am so grateful He has transformed this part of me!

Summers were filled with work and fun. The backpacking trips into the High Sierra with my dad stand out as the high points of my summers in high school. We had a favorite spot in the Ten Lakes region of Yosemite. We would hike into a base camp at around ten thousand feet and then visit and fish all the lakes of that area for about ten days.

Backpacking seemed to me to be the quintessential outdoor experience: surrounded by the breathtaking wilderness by ourselves, the two of us working together, fishing, telling stories around the camp fire…. It required careful planning and great physical exertion, and we felt a great sense of joy and accomplishment when we completed the adventure. Sometimes we encountered bears or rain storms or precipitous rock slides. But every trip created its own special set of memories we could talk about throughout the rest of the year.

When school was out each summer, I would start searching for ways to earn money. At first it was berry picking or yard care. But as I got older and stronger, I started begging Dad to let me work on his construction jobs. I think it was the summer between my sophomore and junior year when he finally acquiesced: "OK, Ron, it's time for you to work with the carpentry crews. But first I want you to demonstrate that you're ready for it by doing a project for me here at home." He went on to explain that the leach line on our septic system had become saturated and needed to be replaced. He wanted me to do the whole job: dig the trench, order gravel and pipe, install it all in the new trench and then hook it up to the tank full of… well, you know what. And dad gave me clear instructions on how to do the job.

I did the whole project in about four days. It was hard work but fun, and quite educational, to say the least. I mentioned earlier that I learn from my mistakes. Well, on this job I made a serious mistake (one I have never made again!). Dad had me do the figuring on how much gravel to order from the local trucking company. I carefully measured the length and width of the trench and multiplied it times the depth of drain rock which yielded the volume in cubic feet. Then I called the gravel company. They sold the material by the cubic *yard*. So, while on the phone, I quickly divided my number by nine and made the order.

An enormous dump truck full of rock soon arrived, backed up the driveway and dumped a huge pile of drain rock next to my project. I sized it up and thought, "*Wow, that's a lot of rock.*" And as the driver was handing me the delivery slip to sign, he matter-of-factly mentioned that the other two trucks were right behind him and would be there momentarily. I was mortified! It suddenly dawned on me that there are twenty-seven cubic feet in a cubic yard, not nine. I had to sheepishly wave off the other two trucks and pay a fine for sending them back to their supply yard. In the years which have followed, I have ordered scores of loads of materials which were sold by the cubic yard—especially concrete—and every time, I have double checked my numbers to make sure I divided by twenty-seven. What a valuable lesson I learned "out in the trenches."

I shoveled the rock into the trench, assembled the perforated pipe, covered it with tar paper and then closed it up with dirt. All that was left was the delightful task of cutting into the old line and connecting it to the new one. I put on knee high rain boots and gingerly sawed the old pipe. Suddenly, with a terrifying gush, I was greeted by a flood of... well, you know what. I hadn't left room in the trench for it, and it flowed all over the place including into my boots. It was my baptism by... well, you know what. It launched my construction career. Twelve years later when I was hanging out my shingle to launch my business as a handyman in Dallas, the very first job which "happened" to come my way was to replace a sewer lateral between a house and the street. Not only was it my Dallas baptism by... well, you know what, but it also had the added charm of being rain-soaked, muddy "gumbo" soil which sticks like glue to the shovel!

To this day I grin as I recall God's wisdom in teaching me humility as I learned how to work. After successfully passing that septic system test, Dad put me out with the crews building houses and small commercial projects. Of course, my first tasks were menial labor: picking up wood blocks, bent nails, and cigarette butts for the trash. But each summer I progressed, and I moved up from carrying the materials, digging footings, pounding stakes and such low level tasks to actually cutting blocks with the cut-off saw and nailing them between the joists. The summer between high school and college I actually helped frame walls and load rafters. I loved it. As it turned out, the skills I learned working for my dad would carry me all the way through my life up until this present moment. My hands have happily borne cuts and bruises and splinters most of my adult life! God has used my building skills to bless my family, my church, and a host of friends.

Since I wasn't an athlete, student government drew my attention. I got my feet wet as junior class commissioner representing my classmates on the student council. That went pretty well, so as that year drew to a close, I decided to run for a school-wide office on the student council. I was thinking about college, and I knew it would look really good on my college applications if I could say I was the Student Body Vice President of Soquel High School. From my experience on the council as a commissioner, I knew that vice president was a name-only position with no public involvement and no tasks to perform. The V.P. simply attended meetings, whereas the Student Body President had to be popular with the whole school and preside over many school-wide events. So I threw my hat into the ring, put up a couple posters around the campus, and what do you know? I got elected V.P. It would look great on my resume. And my classmate named Bob, a very popular natural leader, was elected President.

The following summer (between junior and senior year) was filled with work on the construction jobs, church youth group activities (my entire social life), camping, and proudly driving my '58 Chevrolet Biscayne around Santa Cruz. As the fall term approached, I realized my last chance to prove my manhood as an athlete would soon slip away unless I acted immediately. In those days, there were three levels of football: Varsity (the big boys), Junior Varsity (the younger big boys), and Lightweights (designed primarily for scrawny freshmen). To qualify for Lightweights, you had to pass a weigh-in before each game proving you weighed less than 160 pounds. Well, I saw my chance. No other seniors tried out for lightweights, but I did. I decided I would aim at playing offensive center. It didn't require ball-carrying skill or running, just blocking and snapping the ball to the quarterback (and an occasional long snap to the punter). My self-perceived rite of passage into manhood involved my willingness to bang bodies with the other boys. To my delight, after a painful grapefruit diet, I made the weigh-in and made starting center! I was the lone senior playing with mostly freshmen and a few sophomores. I loved the physicality, and I relished the moments when I would wind up at the bottom of "the pile" of bodies after a play. The pads and helmet were magical protections!

Well, one evening after I came home from football practice, Mom said the school principal had called and wanted to talk with me. Of course, you know my immediate response: *"What did I do wrong?"*

But I muscled up the courage the next day and returned his call. He said, "Congratulations, Ron. You are Soquel High's Student Body President this year!"

I was incredulous. I asked him to explain. He informed me they had asked Bob to resign because his girlfriend was expecting their baby, and that would be an unacceptable embarrassment for the school. So I swallowed a huge lump and began imagining myself as the one leading rallies in the quad and assemblies in the gym, not to mention all the Student Council meetings. I was so glad I had made the football team, because at least I would have a modicum of respect as an athlete.

So my senior year was not what I had expected, but it went well. I filled in as Student Body President as best I could, but I certainly was not the charismatic leader Bob would have been. I didn't go to dances (because my parents and church didn't approve), so I missed out on a lot of activities which would have connected me to the student body. But I loved playing football and treasured my letterman's jacket, which I was awarded. I wore it with a sense of great pride and newfound assurance that I was indeed a man. Academically I was grappling with calculus, physics, and the like. Amazingly, I did well enough in my four years of high school to be selected as the co-valedictorian of my class, so I gave a speech at graduation. Whereas I had begun high school as a small, somewhat annoying, pre-pubescent, non-athletic kid who didn't know what a jock strap even was, as I lived out my senior year, I started to perceive of myself as a BMOC (big man on campus). My female friends in the church youth group even thought it was cool to be seen with me riding in my Chevy.

But as I look back on the opportunity God dropped in my lap that year, I totally missed my chance to take a stand for Jesus. It was the sixties. The civil rights issue was on everyone's tongue. It was the time of "flowers in your hair and free love" in San Francisco. The Viet Nam war was heating up. I was handed a golden opportunity to shine the light of Jesus among my classmates, but I failed because down inside I was ashamed. I never said a peep publically about my faith. And, believe it or not, it would have been permitted at that time. Within a year or two, such open doors slammed shut as public schools became hostile to anything Christian. In retrospect, I realize my silence resulted from the fact that I had no real personal faith. I was simply an excellent specimen of the "Baptist church culture of the 1960s" which meant that I behaved well and avoided foul language, drinking, dancing, and premarital sex. But there was no life-transforming connection between me and the living God. This issue of my personal faith would reach a crisis in my second year of college.

But before God could create a hunger in me for a genuine life-altering faith in Jesus, He needed to expose the ugly sinfulness in me. I *had* to see I wasn't as good as I perceived myself to be. That happened as I left home and began my first year of college.

3

Westmont College—Ugly Exposure

It was early September 1964. I packed up my Chevy with my clothes and my guitar and headed down Highway 101 to Santa Barbara. Dad waved a parting gesture of approbation, while Mom shed tears of sadness because Ronnie was leaving home. Dad was also wincing from the pain of paying my tuition. He had been ruefully confronted with the frustrating situation that—despite my high academic performance in high school—I didn't receive any scholarships because "he owned property." Most of the property was in transition for development, but the scholarship granters didn't care.

I had followed the advice of my church leaders to enroll in a Christian school. I think I primarily chose Westmont because I would know one person on campus, my partner from "Dirty Dave & Rotten Ron." But very quickly it would become apparent that Westmont was not a fit for me at all. I was a math and science guy leaning towards engineering, but in 1964, Westmont was strictly a liberal arts school, focused on the social sciences.

I was assigned to a three man room in the men's dormitory. I had never had a roommate, and the adjustment was painful. I was surrounded by rowdy young men who played their music LOUDLY until curfew. And it wasn't my style of music. I loved Christian music and folk music, but they were playing secular rock and roll! My fellow students were very intelligent and had read lots of books. They loved to stay up until all hours of the night (and, of course, I didn't). It was hard to find solitude in my own dorm room. One of my roommates had such a difficult time adjusting to life in the dorm away from home that he dropped out at the end of the fall term and went home.

But I'm grateful to God for my year at Westmont. I honestly gave it my best shot, but the academics were just not clicking with me. I had been the self-perceived BMOC at Soquel High School, but now I was surrounded by people with much more talent and leadership skills than I. But God used Westmont to dramatically expose the raw, self-centered, sinner I was.

Only three days into the fall semester, that part of Montecito was upended by the devastating Coyote wildfire which raged right next to the campus. It would burn up the steep slopes above the campus during the day and then turn around and blast its way back down towards the campus at night, driven by powerful Santa Ana winds. It ultimately destroyed two buildings on campus during its three-day run. On the first night of the fire, my roommate Dale and I decided we wanted to be helpful, so we hiked up the hill to the line which was being held by the firefighters. Try to picture us— young guys in ordinary clothes with no training in firefighting.... We wandered for a few minutes amid the fire trucks and hoses while the actual firemen were out on the line challenging the crackling flames about a hundred feet away. We were in the middle of trying to figure out what we could do to help when a huge oak tree about twenty feet from us suddenly exploded into flames! It scared the you-know-what out of us. The heat and fury were so intense that we instinctively bolted, and I ran just about as fast as I've ever run in my life! So much for our desire to be heroes. That night I gained an instant respect and appreciation for the work firefighters do, and I learned how awful wildfires are. In the years which have followed, my path has intersected with several devastating wildfires, and each time my memory has catapulted me back to the burning oak tree in Montecito in September 1964.

I also learned one other thing from that fire: what fear feels like. I had lived a pretty sheltered and serene life for the first eighteen years. I had never felt fear grip my gut like that night when the oak exploded in my face—even when I was shot with a shotgun. In an instant I knew I was dead if I remained more than a few moments in that inferno. In retrospect, I am grateful for that moment of sudden dread and fear. It pried open what has become a deep and worshipful fountain of appreciation for each moment of life God has given me ever since. I know how fragile life can be, and I want to make sure I honor the One who gave it to me.

Life at Westmont was good—partly because it was Santa Barbara! But I never seemed to mesh with the social life of the school. I did, however, thoroughly enjoy my stint with the touring college chorale under the direction of Dr. John Lundberg. I learned how to sing genuine choral music. But my social studies classes just didn't mesh with my interests. I found psychology quite dull. Of course, I became great friends with my roommate Dale. He got a job working in a local avocado orchard and would bring us bags of freshly picked fruit to eat in our room on crackers we pirated from the dining commons. During the second semester Dale and I were joined by a new roommate named Fred. The three of us became great pals, and Dale and Fred became willing accomplices in the nefarious deed I hatched in the spring of '65.

My spiritual life at Westmont was nothing more than superficial. I adapted to the norms and behaviors of my peers so that I wouldn't stand out. As I have said, I was the good Baptist kid who followed the church crowd, but nothing was springing from within. I had no interest in the things which mark a genuine follower of Jesus. So I sat through chapels and Bible classes without allowing them to touch my heart. However, one chapel totally got my attention. Normally, everything was coed at Westmont. But on this one particular day, the men and women were divided, and we each heard a sex talk from a medical professional in Santa Barbara. The urologist was there to tell us how they treated what were then called venereal diseases. (Now they're called sexually transmitted diseases because "venereal" means immoral conduct which is no longer considered politically correct.) I can still see the doc in his white coat telling us about his treatment for syphilis. He described a roto-rooter-like instrument he would insert into the male's penis. Then he would open the blades and rotate it as he pulled it out to clean out the blockages caused by the disease. He asked, "Is it worth it to have premarital sex, men?"

I remember squirming in my seat and screaming silently, "*NO!*" I don't remember any other chapel service at Westmont, but that one stuck. At that point in my life I didn't have a spiritual reason to remain pure before marriage, but God graciously used my dislike of pain (particularly in that region of my anatomy!) to keep me chaste. I remember more than one occasion when I was later tempted to "experiment," and I walked away because I could feel the roto-rooter.

There was a young woman in my freshman class named Carol. She had soft, reddish brown hair, a wonderful smile, and she spoke with a captivating Pennsylvania accent. I would see her in class, and my heart would go pitter patter. One day in late winter I muscled up courage to ask her to a special college event. To my great delight, she accepted. So I planned an evening to impress. I took her to one of the fanciest restaurants in that part of the state, and we had a wonderful evening together. She sat close to me on the wide bench seat of my '58 Chevy. I began to have sweet memories of my last days at Soquel High when I was a BMOC. I began to dream that perhaps "she was the one." I didn't have courage to ask her out again for a few weeks until the college announced their major spring formal involving an extravagant dinner theater at a country club in Montecito. Everybody who was anybody at Westmont was going, so I had a burning desire to be there with Carol. I pictured myself in my tuxedo (acquired for choir tour) walking in with Carol on my arm in her frilly spring formal gown.

The day came when our paths crossed on campus, and I had my chance to ask her to go with me. My heart was beating out of my chest as I squeaked out, "Carol, I'd be honored to have you go with me to the spring formal. Would you?"

There was a moment of silence, and then she said, "I'm sorry, Ron. I'm already going with Larry so-and-so."

I politely responded, "Oh, OK, thanks," but I was crushed. I sulked back to my dorm room to brood over my failure. "*How could she ever want to go with that big, fat, ugly guy?*" I thought. "*I can't believe she'd go with him.*" As I ruminated over this awful blow to my young male ego, revenge began accumulating in my heart like dripping acid. I told my roommates. They felt sorry for me, but they had no idea how deeply my anger was burning inside. It only took me a couple days to hatch my revenge. I would make Larry and Carol regret they attended that dinner together.

I was a fledgling math and science student and had become familiar with the usage of Greek letters in formulae. I didn't know a single word of Greek, just the letters used in the various equations and formulae. I picked three letters I liked and dubbed myself "The ΠΔΦ"—*pie delta phee*. About two weeks before the big dinner, I wrote out a note which couldn't be identified as from me and mailed it to Carol. It said, "Beware of the ΠΔΦ." I had a cousin in a distant city mail it so that the postmark was from far away.

The featured play at the spring dinner theater was performed by the local troupe from the Westmont drama department. The school wanted to make sure that everyone on campus could see the play, even if they didn't attend the formal dinner theater on Saturday. So they opened the country club up to anyone who would like to see the dress rehearsal on Friday. I talked with my roommates, and they decided to join me in my revengeful endeavor. So we "cased the joint" on the night before the big affair ostensibly to see the rehearsal. I was in luck. The volunteers were quietly getting the place all decorated while the play was going on. They were putting out elaborately lettered name cards for each couple. My roomies and I discreetly searched the tables and found Larry and Carol's. We sat there while we "watched the play" and waited for a moment when everyone's attention was on the stage, and then I quickly pulled out my Sharpie pen and marked ΠΔΦ on their name cards. No one noticed. So far so good. As soon as the play was over, we buzzed home and began making plans for Saturday night.

In my preparations, I had acquired four cement blocks, a car jack, some Vaseline, a bar of soap, and a device to release air from tires. I had carefully studied Larry's car and learned his license number. On Friday night, we had scoped out the parking area of the country club, and it was very amenable to our plan. We knew what time guests would start arriving. So my roomies and I arrived about a half hour before. We found a very agreeable configuration of shrubs in which to hide as we watched cars begin to arrive. Sure enough, here came Larry and Carol. They were double-dating, so the two gentlemen in penguin suits jumped out and opened the doors for their formally attired dates. Carol had gotten her hair fixed. She looked beautiful. The men ushered their dates into the dining hall. My heart was pounding, partly for the excitement of the conquest and partly because someone might arrive late and catch us in the act. Fortunately, no one saw us. We waited until we knew dinner was well underway, and then we sprang into action.

We systematically went around the car jacking up each wheel, then letting the axels back down on the concrete blocks. This left the car about a quarter inch off the ground. Once on blocks, we let the air out of all four tires. Then for a greeting, with the bar of soap, I wrote in big letters ΠΔΦ on the windshield. As the crew was finishing up, I smeared a large dab of clear Vaseline on the driver's door handle. Then we retreated to our hiding place to watch the fireworks. Everything worked to a T. The two couples came joyfully out to their car, and the gentlemen let the ladies into their seats. Then ugly Larry grabbed his door handle and got a fist full of Vaseline. He shouted out a curse word. One of the ladies had a handkerchief, and Larry cleaned his hands. Then he slid into the car and let out another curse word as he saw ΠΔΦ on the windshield. So after a few minutes of cleaning the windshield, he got back in and started the car. He put it in gear and… the wheels just spun.

Larry and his buddy jumped out of the car, this time with multiple curse words. They looked under the car and discovered the concrete blocks. After a few more curse words, they extricated the jack from its niche in the trunk and began jacking up the car to remove the concrete blocks, only to realize that when the car came back down it was sitting on four flat tires. Now Larry and his buddy were livid. Their dates had a curfew, and they were going to be late (and they were). My roomies and I decided we had seen enough of the show, and it was time to get out of there before we got caught. So we slipped away unnoticed and drove back to the dorm congratulating each other on how well everything had gone. We had been a great team. We were amazed that everything had gone exactly as conceived. No slip-ups. And we didn't get caught.

I went to bed that night re-living the scene of Larry cursing a blue streak when the car settled down on flat tires. Revenge felt so good. I had made them regret they went to the dinner, just as I intended. This was better than playing football last year.

But then everything fell apart. Unbeknownst to me, a hatchet murderer was on the loose somewhere along the east coast, and he had already killed two young college co-eds. And when he did the deed, he left his calling card: ΠΔΘ! The slight difference between Φ and Θ seemed trivial, and the local authorities had ordered Westmont's girls' dormitory into full lock-down mode, surmising that the killer had found his way to the west coast.

When I heard the news, I was sick in the pit of my stomach. My little "controlled burn" had suddenly become a raging forest fire. I sequestered myself in my room while I sent my roomies out to see if they could find out what was happening on campus. Slowly I got wind that the dean had decided he wouldn't release the lock-down until he had talked to every male student on campus to see what information each might have about finding the perpetrator of this vicious prank. So Dr. Hillegas began a systematic pursuit of information, as a parade of male students lined up outside his office. My roommates agreed to lie for me. Westmont was abuzz with gossip about this awful perpetrator (me!), and what was being said is not fit to print here. Yet, no one on campus knew who was responsible except Dale, Fred and me.

As the time for my appointment with Dr. Hillegas drew near, I was in agony. I knew I just needed to say I didn't know anything about it, and he would move on to the next guy. In time everything would blow over, and I would be out of the woods, although I would have to come to terms with a screaming guilty conscience. I also knew I didn't lie well. For eighteen years my parents had taught me to always tell the truth. As I walked into the dean's office that day, I still wasn't sure what I was going to say. Then he looked me in the eye and popped the question: "Ron, we're asking every student what they know about the situation at the spring dinner last Saturday. I'm sure you've heard about the ΠΔΦ, and the fear over Carol _____'s well-being. Do you know anything about it?"

As he was speaking, I quickly realized he had absolutely no suspicion of my involvement. For a moment I saw daylight. I could walk free, and never look back.

But I confessed. From this vantage point, as I write many years later, I can clearly see that it was the work of the Holy Spirit in my life. He wanted me to bear the pain of having the filthy ugliness exposed which lay hidden deep inside this self-perceived good church kid. "The heart is more deceitful than all else and is desperately sick," says the Word of God (Jeremiah 17:9, NASB). I felt the shame of seeing the wickedness of my own vengeful heart. Mature perspective has shown me that, had I continued on that path of gleeful undercover, anger-driven misconduct, I could have easily ended up doing prison time as a full-on criminal.

Dr. Hillegas was visibly relieved. And after perceiving my remorse, he reminded me of the seriousness of my actions and that Carol's parents could press charges for threatening her life. And then he added, "I'm only going to ask you to do one thing. Call Carol and tell her you are going to come to her dorm and apologize to her face to face."

"Please, Dr. Hillegas," I pleaded, "I'll pull weeds around the campus till school's out, but not that." I shuddered at the idea of looking into the eyes of the one whom I had hurt so badly with my vengeful anger.

But I did it. It was the hardest thing I had done in my life up until then. As I faced Carol across the table in the foyer of the women's dorm, she plaintively asked, "Why did you do it, Ron?"

"I don't know," I said. "I guess I'm just a rotten apple."

Word spread like a wildfire around campus—and we didn't even have social media! From that moment until the close of the semester (about a month), I was the campus goat. I would slink into the dining commons, grab my food and disappear into my dorm room. I only appeared on campus to walk between classes, speaking to no one. It's amazing to me now that I even finished out the year. I couldn't wait for school to be out.

I drove home with Santa Barbara permanently etched in the rear view mirror of my life. I told my dear parents nothing of the incident. I only said I had decided that

Westmont didn't work out for me, and I wanted to transfer to an engineering school. I had already applied and been accepted as a transfer student at LeTourneau College in Texas. But the harsh reality was that the BMOC who entered Westmont in the fall, left Westmont the next spring as a beaten dog with his tail between his legs.

When God wants to do a work of grace in a man's life, He has to begin with a broken ego. Mine started breaking in Santa Barbara. I was still the church kid—only now with a haunting, palpable awareness of the ugly sinfulness within me.

4

LeTourneau College—Crisis of Faith

Back home in Santa Cruz (summer of '65), I tried to resume life as though nothing had ever happened. For quite a while I lived with the dread that the police authorities were going to arrest me for threatening Carol's life, but evidently her parents never decided to press charges. And my friend Dave— the only liaison between Westmont and my life in Santa Cruz—kept his mouth sealed about the whole incident. God was gracious, enabling me to resume my former life at home: working as a carpenter's apprentice and driving around in a vintage 1930 Model A Ford which I bought from my next door neighbor. The girls loved riding in the rumble seat. And I began to prepare for my move to Longview, Texas.

Dad helped me sell the Model A and buy a low mileage Volvo, and I headed off for Longview in mid-August with the hope of starting all over. After the long hot drive across the arid West Texas plains, I pulled into a motel in Longview. I got settled into my room, and I headed for the swimming pool to cool off. There was one other man in the pool. While I dunked and swam laps and generally allowed the water to restore my weary body, he started talking to me. I wasn't the least bit interested in returning his chatter. But with careful calculations, as he talked he kept inching his way toward me and backing me up into a corner of the pool. One I was cornered, he kept moving closer until he was within arm's length. All at once I saw his right arm dip under the water and start moving toward my groin. I was totally naïve to the tactics of a homosexual predator, and at first I was confused: "*What does he think he's doing?*" And then with lightning speed I realized he was about to reach into my bathing suit and grab my genitals. In retrospect I realize that God's Spirit was protecting me and my virginity *again*. I flailed his arm to the side and hollered: "You keep away from me!" Like Joseph fleeing from the advances of Potiphar's wife, I jumped out of the pool and ran up to my room, locking the door behind me. Welcome to Longview.

I enrolled at LeTourneau, and very quickly I knew it was a better fit. The engineering courses resonated with my natural bent as a budding "geek." I loved solving problems and, in God's grace, did exceptionally well in all my classes. I was assigned residence with the young men of Lamda Alpha Sigma (ΛΑΣ—LeTourneau Aviation Society) because I had declared my intent to major in Aeronautical Engineering. It was natural for me to pledge the fraternity. All the other brothers were Aerotech majors, studying for their Airframe and Powerplant license to repair aircraft. Most all of them were also learning to fly. We ate, drank, and talked aviation. So it was natural that by the time I graduated, I had earned my private pilot rating and was able to rent a Piper Cherokee at the airport and take friends out for rides.

One warm autumn evening, I was sitting outside my dorm and heard the alluring sounds of someone singing folk music accompanied by a 12-string guitar being played quite well. So I wandered over to meet the guy responsible. His name was Bob Johnson. He was from North Carolina and had the drawl to prove it. He played great folk music, and I liked him from the outset. He invited me to get my guitar and join him in a little jam. It was fun to sing with him, but it didn't take me long to figure out that he was *way* better on the guitar than I was. So he floated an audacious idea: "Hey Ron, I was in the music store in Longview the other day and saw a broken stand-up bass in two pieces collecting dust in the back room. I'll bet you could buy it cheap, fix it up, and we could form a music group with a co-ed I'm getting to know named Maxine. She plays the tambourine!"

Next thing you know, I had bought the broken instrument for $50 along with a book on how to play it. I figured out how to glue the thing back together, installed a bridge and tailpiece, and stretched new strings on it. The old veteran looked rather pathetic, all scratched-up and scuffed-up. But it created great folk style "thumps," and in just a few days The Woodlunders were born. I took to the bass quite naturally because since early days, I had always "heard" the bass line in my head whenever I sang. I crafted a nifty homemade rack for the top of my Volvo, and when the Woodlunders would go out on the road, we would tool down the highway with the bass perched on the top, scrolled neck hanging out over the front windshield. We quickly became known around town and performed for Longview civic groups, nearby junior colleges and the LeTourneau chapel. One of our last gigs was the second annual LeTourneau Homecoming Hootenanny.

Speaking of that Hootenanny in 1966.... Forty-nine years later, the Woodlunders regathered once again (Bob and Maxine came from Florida, and I came from California) to perform for the Fiftieth Anniversary Hootenanny. We were invited to reprise some old tunes as the featured remnants of the early days of the Hootenanny. Only instead of the youthful, handsome, slim trio of 1966, this time we were aging, sagging, widening, wrinkling, and graying veterans. But Bob was still able to deliver the solo riff on "Walk Right In" without missing a note. It truly was a memorable moment to be in the spotlight on that grand stage and perform for two thousand people in the new LeTourneau concert hall.

But in 1965, I was still a man in formation, and the process was at times shambolic. One thinks one has established his adult identity, when an unexpected event suddenly reveals otherwise. Such was the case the day I was driving the blue Volvo with the four-on-the-floor into town for some errands. All at once the car started bucking and then came to an abrupt stop. I was just barely able to get it to the side of the road. The transmission had frozen up, and there was nothing I could do. I got out of the car and noticed a phone booth a short distance away. I walked to the phone booth and placed a collect call to my dad who was sitting at his construction desk in Santa Cruz. "Hey Dad! My Volvo broke down. What should I do?" By that I *meant*, "What are *you* going to do?"

Dad calmly chatted with me for a moment, feeling sorry for my predicament. Then he said, "Don't they have towing companies and repair shops in Longview?"

I remember the chill that went through my body as I suddenly saw myself as little Ronnie looking up at big daddy and asking him to fix my problem. I grew up in that instant as I responded, "Thanks, Dad. Yes. I'll take care of it. Give my love to Mom." I handled it from there without his help. And I am eternally grateful to God for Dad's wisdom which gently facilitated my maturing into independent manhood.

LeTourneau was a solidly Christian college, and we had regular chapel services. But as I listened to the various speakers, I found myself slowly coming to the realization that what they talked about was not real to me. Christianity was simply my culture but not my faith. Were its tenets even true? Was Christianity just a particular lifestyle which seemed to make some people feel good, but with no more validity than any other chosen lifestyle? I was at the age where the world was beckoning to me like the doorman outside a Bourbon Street bar, inviting me to indulge in its pleasurable deeds. My ingrained habits of so-called Christianity forbade my participation, but why was I restricting myself? If a girl offered herself to me, would I partake? If not, why not? If I didn't really believe the Bible stuff, why not indulge in anything I felt I wanted? Sure, I had had a religious experience of feeling sinful when I was six. Sure, I felt guilt for the unfortunate consequences of my bitter revenge against Carol. But secular psychology describes guilt totally unrelated to any true spiritual presence of sin. I came to the stark awareness that my so-called faith was greatly restricting my choices in life, and if it wasn't even real, I was a fool to miss out on the pleasures the big wide world had to offer. I was ready to let go of my faith and follow my own thinking and desires. I was pretty smart on my own, and I could certainly navigate my way through my life without any so-called god raining on my parade.

But there was this nagging thought that wouldn't leave my mind: *"What if Christianity IS right? If it is, then I will suffer the consequences of my sin and ultimately perish in hell."* I knew John 3:16-18. I had memorized it on my bed early in the morning when I was nine:

> "For God so loved the world, that He gave His only begotten Son, that whoever believes in Him shall not perish, but have eternal life. For God did not send the Son into the world to judge the world, but that the

world might be saved through Him. He who believes in Him is not judged; he who does not believe has been judged already, because he has not believed in the name of the only begotten Son of God" (NASB).

In my academic studies I was learning the scientific method of solving problems. We were taught to make sure that we had assembled and accounted for all the "givens" before we pulled together our solution. Wanting to be a good engineer, I applied this principle to the problem of my doubts about Christianity. I realized it was premature to throw out my faith if I wasn't sure of its validity. I needed some way to objectively prove it was wrong, and then I could happily and freely dismiss it. I could live confidently in my unbelief or agnosticism. I would be the captain of my own ship.

Here's where God lovingly intervened in my life *again*. While caught in this whirling vortex—this crisis of my faith—I ran into one of the professors, Dr. Bill Nix, who had taken a liking to me because he liked the music of the Woodlunders. I threw my quandary at him, and he listened attentively. Then he said, "Ron, before you jettison your faith, I encourage you to read a couple books about the scientific case for the resurrection of Jesus."

And then he mentioned *Who Moved the Stone*, by Frank Morrison and *Evidence That Demands a Verdict*, by Josh McDowell. He walked me to his office and handed the books to me. I will be eternally grateful to Dr. Nix.

No one had ever shown me there were clear, objective, historical, scientific and irrefutable evidences for the fact that Jesus came back to life. Christianity had always been presented as something to choose to believe—much like kids are told to believe in Santa. I knew that, although some people believed it very strongly, their belief didn't make it true. Others said their faith was true because they could feel it deep within themselves. This sentiment was driven home in the hymn we often sang in church called "He Lives." It contained the vacuous line: "You ask me how I know He lives—He lives within my heart." I knew that many people of many religious persuasions felt very deeply about their faith—but that didn't make what they believed true. Faith as I perceived it was totally subjective, whatever each person of faith wanted it to be.

But when I started reading Morrison and McDowell, I began to learn, much to my amazement, that there were multiple lines of courtroom-worthy evidence documenting a clear death-defying miracle. Jesus' resurrection was a manifest fact on par with the reality of gravity or the rotation of the earth or Newton's laws of motion. I accepted those realities and ordered my life accordingly. Would I order my life on the fact of the resurrection of Jesus? I began to see that Christianity was not merely make-believe. How could I dismiss it from my life since it was premised on a documented reality?

As I read (and talked with Dr. Nix), I came to see that the resurrection is indeed the watershed for all issues in Christianity. Since Jesus came back to life just as He claimed He would, all His other (often seemingly outrageous) claims must also be true. Actually, what He says about *any* matter must be true. Without the resurrection, Christianity is merely a fairy tale. With the resurrection, it is the path to life and hope for all of eternity. This young engineering student slowly came to terms with this monumental idea. I was boxed in by the "givens" of undeniable truth.

I remember the day when I went to my dorm room and had a serious long talk with Jesus. I told Him I was ready to freshly commit my life to Him because I was convinced He had risen from the dead. I said I was ready to quit conforming to the Christian culture around me and start directly obeying what He asked of me in His Word. I confessed my ugly, vengeful sinfulness which had been on graphic display the year before at Westmont, and I asked Him to root it out of me. I told Him that He was worth more than any earthly pleasure I might be forfeiting. I confessed that I was very young and naïve in "the faith," and I promised to embark on a journey of growing. And the last thing I asked came deep from my heart, "Lord, I know in my head that You are alive. I'm convinced of the proofs. But I need to see evidences that You are alive in me right now. I need to see You do supernatural things that I couldn't make happen on my own. I want to see You unmistakably at work in my life." Little did I know at that moment how He was about to launch me on an adventure of miraculous happenings which would characterize my life from that day to the very present as I write these words!

That was the mid-spring of 1966. I felt like a new man. I had a brand-new love for the scriptures and found myself opening the Bible to understand and apply it to my life. For the first time, the multitude of Biblical truths I had learned from my parents and church experiences started making sense and having life-transforming meaning. Scriptures learned by rote many years before started springing to life in my mind. I was a true believer in Jesus now—not a phony nice-guy-church-kid.

I had a hunger to use my time to further His kingdom, and I found my earthly desires being changed. The most glaring example of this was my TV. When I moved from Santa Cruz to Longview the previous August, my little Volvo proudly transported a gift from my mother: a slick little black and white TV designed for college dorms. I had built a little shelf for it above my bureau and wired up a "remote control"—a switch to turn it on and off from my bed. It was pretty sweet—part of the college dorm room shtick. It was my long-time habit (from early days at home with my family) to walk into the room and automatically turn on the TV to see what I was missing. Often it would captivate me for a considerable length of time. As I started reading the scriptures I encountered the verse which says, "Therefore be careful how you walk, not as unwise men but as wise, making the most of your time, because the days are evil" (Ephesians 5:15-16, NASB). The Spirit of God started making me feel very uncomfortable about the time I was wasting watching TV. It was accomplishing nothing except filling me with thoughts which were contrary to godliness. Finally, I said, "OK, Lord, I'll get rid of the TV and devote my time fully to You." I took the TV down from its shelf and hauled it to the Gregg County landfill. God was beginning to miraculously purify my thought life and sensitize me to the evil thinking of the world. TV left my life that day in the spring of 1966, and it has never found its way back.

In those days LeTourneau College was dominated by men. There were about a thousand male students and thirty young women. The pool of dating opportunities on campus was pretty shallow! This was a blessing because it enabled me to pursue my studies with minimal distractions. But I did find time on a couple occasions to date young women I met at church in town. Since I was committed to growing in my new life as a full-on follower of Jesus, I was eager to find meaningful spiritual conversations with the girls I dated. But it was not to be. My sample of the Longview data was not productive at all. The girls were cute southern belles—sappy sweet, nicely made up with every hair in place, but devoid of serious conversations *on any subject*. I was used to engaging dialog with my college peers and professors. One day as I was meeting with the Lord, it became apparent to me that dating was obscuring my new love for Jesus. So I made a pledge to Him that, during this early phase of my spiritual growth, I was simply going to stop looking around and focus entirely on Him. Dating hadn't worked at Westmont. It wasn't working in Longview. If He had a woman for me, He was going to have to bring her into my life through miraculous circumstances.

Within days of that promise to God, I was sitting in chapel listening to a guest speaker named Paul Bubar. He was a wiry, energetic, animated guy who was on campus recruiting counselors for a teenage camp called Word of Life in the far away Adirondack mountains of New York. With infectious enthusiasm he spoke of the opportunity they would provide to any of us who would give them the next summer. They would not only teach us how to be counselors, but they would also teach us how to grow spiritually and study the Bible in depth. And it would all take place on an island paradise in the middle of a gorgeous lake surrounded by birch forests.

For the first time in my new life in Christ, my ears were opened to the voice of God. He spoke quite clearly to me: "Ron, this is for you."

I couldn't wait for the meeting to be dismissed. I ran to the front, signed up with Mr. Bubar, and started making plans for the summer in upstate New York. When I got back to my dorm, I had a time of great rejoicing in prayer. I gushed: "Thank You, Lord, for this wonderful opportunity You have created—seemingly just for me! I promise You that this is about my growth. I am hungry to learn how to live my faith and serve You. And please help me keep my recent pledge to not pursue dating girls."

At that moment I realized that, just weeks before, I had asked Him to show me that the resurrected Jesus was alive and working miracles *today*. And He was just getting started. I called my parents and let them know they would only see me for a brief visit after school was out because I would be at Word of Life for the summer.

5

Word of Life—Cathy

After classes were finished in the spring of '66, I made a quick visit back to Santa Cruz. The Volvo got repaired in Longview, but it was showing signs of its age, so Dad helped me trade it in on a shiny new Ford Mustang. It was sweet, with power to burn. Great car for a young buck. I drove it proudly back down to Longview, picked up my gear for the summer, and then drove to Schroon Lake, New York. As I said, the camp was on an island, so they had a big staging area/parking lot on the mainland of Schroon Lake where I parked and waited for the ferry. Others were also gathering to wait for the ferry. I knew no one, of course, so I began to introduce myself. It was fascinating to meet people from all over the east. One car arrived with Massachusetts plates, and I was drawn to the petite brown-haired girl who jumped out, grabbed her things, and made her way to the dock to wait. Just as the ferry was docking, I went over and introduced myself. "Hi, I'm Ron from California."

"Hi, I'm Cathy from Boston."

Those first words electrified me. She spoke with an accent I had never heard before except from President John Kennedy. I was fascinated, but I was *not* going to look at girls! I had made God a solemn promise. So as the ferry chugged across the mile of open water, I focused on the gorgeous scenery and imagined what the summer was going to be like as I learned all God was going to teach me. Once on the island, I got established in my cabin, learned the routines which we were going to follow, and generally settled in for an adventure. The first week was "get ready for the campers week." That meant training classes in the morning and work details around the island cleaning up from the winter storms in the afternoons. We immediately embarked on a series of classes on Bible study methods with a man named Howard Hendricks. I had never even heard of him, but was soon to learn he was an internationally acclaimed teacher. And he was teaching our little group of ten counselors. I was thrilled with what I started learning, and I was quickly seeing how God had definitely designed this just for me.

One afternoon I "happened" to be assigned to the same work detail as "Cathy from Boston" whom I had met at the dock a few days before. We were directed to clean up the area around the big campfire circle which was littered with huge logs that had been knocked around by the winter storms. While most of the crew were raking up piles of debris, I decided to display my manly strength by picking up thirty-inch diameter logs and carrying them away by myself. I waited until "Cathy from Boston" seemed to be looking in my direction before I made each trip. I was hopeful of impressing her. But months later when I told her about it, she said she never even noticed! This incident highlighted my conflict. I was there to grow and not to notice girls. I had a serious talk with the Lord about keeping my promise. Little did I know that He was going to use Cathy to spur my spiritual progress!

That summer at Word of Life was absolutely amazing. The speakers and teachers were world-class. The opportunity to learn how to work with young boys in my cabin was foundational to everything that was to follow in my life. Rubbing shoulders with sold-out followers of Christ from all over the U.S. was powerful. I saw living examples of faith. *Every day* I thanked God that Paul Bubar had found his way to *my* college to bring the invitation just at the moment when *I* was ready to fully benefit from it!

But far and away, the most monumental aspect of the summer of '66 on Word of Life Island was the relationship which God had planned for me with "Cathy from Boston." One day during our second week on the island, we were in a meeting together. People were sharing around the circle, and I heard her talk about her time with Jesus in the Bible that day. She talked like she was a veteran. I was a newbie, and it was magnetic for me. I was drawn to a woman who was so intelligent and obviously deeply in love with Jesus. She was the real deal, and I wanted to learn from her. I muscled up courage after the meeting and walked over to her. "Cathy," I asked quite audaciously, "Would you like a Quiet Time partner? I would like to learn from you and with you. Would you be willing to meet me every day so we can talk about our time with Jesus and pray together?"

As I heard myself speaking the words, I was painfully aware how inappropriately forward this was. She literally did not know me from Adam. But then—to my eternal delight— she looked up at me and said, quite sincerely, "I'd like that."

Thus began my daily meetings with Cathy Jean Campbell, the amazing woman who would become my wife of 48 years, mother to our five children, and grandmother to our eight grandchildren. We chose the book of Philippians and worked out a reading schedule right then. The next day we each spent time alone with God in the morning in the first few verses of Philippians 1, and then we met in the afternoon for our sharing time. That continued for the rest of the summer. Each day we met, we entered a step deeper into fellowship with God and with each other. I learned so much about what it was to have an intimate, personal connection with Jesus. As the summer progressed, we gradually fell deeply in love with each other. Cathy even had to send a "Dear John" letter to a young man back in Boston who had assumed she would be his wife.

Now I need to explain that Word of Life had some rather restrictive guidelines for relationships. We were not allowed to touch each other. So we fell deeply in love and knew we were destined to be husband and wife without a moment of physical contact. As I have related that anecdote to people down through the years, most are astounded. Cathy's birthday was the end of July. We had been seeing each other for about five weeks. She was a "junior counselor" because of her age, and I was a "senior counselor," so our schedules and days off were mostly different. But when her birthday was approaching, we managed to arrange for the same day off to leave the island (where the rules about no touching didn't apply) and have dinner together. On an earlier day off I had made a reservation at a nice restaurant in downtown Schroon Lake. When the day came, we rode the ferry back to the mainland and then walked toward the restaurant. While we were busily chatting about how great the summer was going, it suddenly occurred to me that we were *off* the island. So I gently took her hand. Instantly our conversation stopped, all the trees around us turned a deeper green, and we gazed at each other with amazed disbelief. What had happened? We realized God was showing us a foretaste of the joy we would share together for the rest of our life. After the delightful dinner, we sat on a park bench holding hands. I looked at her and said, "Cathy, someday you're going to be my wife."

We kissed, and she just nodded a wistful yes. (For years afterwards, she would tell friends I never proposed; I just announced...!)

We immediately began making plans for our future. Cathy was about to start a three-year nursing program in Boston, and I had two more years of school at LeTourneau. We pledged our faithfulness to each other for the long wait until she had completed nursing school. And we agreed to continue the spiritual connection which had spawned our love. The day I left Schroon Lake to return to college, we started writing *daily* letters (snail mail!) to each other. Those letters were full of old-fashioned connection. They were a mix of newsy chit chat of our daily lives at our respective schools and deep spiritual sharing about what we were learning each day from our synchronized Quiet Times. I believe we had the blessed privilege of getting to know each other much more deeply than most couples ever do before marriage. The letter-writing lasted for two years—that's approximately 1,400 letters! We kept them in a box for fifty years as a sweet monument to the development of our spiritual and soulish oneness.

As Cathy told me more about herself and her story, I came to see how truly remarkable and miraculous it was that God brought us together. Our families of origin were poles (and miles!) apart: She came from an entrenched, inner city, east coast, unbelieving, working class family with five siblings. I grew up on the much looser west coast in an entrepreneurial family of Christians with means and just one sister. I had been around the church all my life; she met the Lord through a radical conversion at age sixteen (only a year and a half before I met her). She had never traveled away from Massachusetts before her trip to Word of Life. She was a brilliant scholar who had skipped a grade in grammar school and excelled in the six-year program in the classics (especially French and Latin) at Boston Girls' Latin School. I was a science and math geek who had barely read twenty books in my life.

But the most amazing piece of our "coincidence" was that she shouldn't even have been at Word of Life that summer! She had applied and been accepted to enter the three-year, round-the-calendar, live-in nursing program at New England Baptist Hospital (NEBH) the year before (1965). But she was told she must wait a whole year because she was too young (having skipped the second grade). So she had to fill up a year waiting for her nursing program to begin. Part of that "filling" was a last minute decision to be a junior counselor at Word of Life. If the nursing school had taken her the previous year, she would have been immersed in the year-round program at NEBH, and our paths would never have crossed. The Jesus who is alive and working miracles today orchestrated the timing so exquisitely that we would literally land on the ferry to the Island at the very same moment! The Lord had answered the prayer I prayed in my dorm room four months earlier with dramatic clarity. My life was abounding with the truth of Ecclesiastes 3:11: "He has made everything beautiful in its time" (NIV).

I had left LeTourneau in June with a heart of expectancy. I returned to LeTourneau in late August with a heart of gratitude and a sense of purpose and direction! God had shown me He cared about me personally, and I was ready to tackle my studies with gusto—and no female distractions! The next two years were filled with hard work and *lots* of reading and writing love letters. The more I got to know Jesus personally through the intake of His word, the more I wanted to model myself after Paul's young disciple named Timothy.

Paul challenged him to fight the good fight of faith by turning away from a love for money and pursuing godliness (1 Timothy 6:9-12). And he called his young warrior "O man of God." This was a natural outgrowth of the verse I had adopted as my life verse with Cathy on the Island: "To me the living of life is Christ and the dying of death is gain" (Philippians 1:21, literal translation of the Greek). As my undergraduate studies climaxed and graduation drew near, I found myself telling God, "I don't want to be an engineer who happens to be a Christian. I want to be a man of God who happens to earn his living as an engineer."

Unfortunately, my experiences with church in the Longview area were not quite as exciting as my experiences with Jesus. My friend Bill Nix got me connected with an opportunity for ministry with a little country congregation called East Sabine Baptist Church. I was hired as the song leader for Sunday services. I waved my hand while the organist and pianist played the old hymns. Sometimes the people sang, sometimes they didn't. It was pretty pathetic, actually. But in the course of getting to know the attendees, I developed a burden for the six or eight high school-aged kids who hung around church but were totally disinterested in spiritual things. I asked if I could be appointed as the youth group leader. The pastor agreed and handed me a booklet published by the denomination. It was a thirteen-week study on the officers of the church: the pastor, the treasurer, the music leader, the kitchen keeper, the Sunday school teachers, etc., ad nauseam. Thirteen weeks of that. I took it home and prayed. I decided to do a one-week lesson touching on all thirteen officers. Then, in the following weeks I led Bible explorations and discussions on dating, sex, self-image, purpose in life, etc. The kids were eating it up. But about six weeks into my new role as youth leader, I was summoned to the pastor's office, where he and his deacons were awaiting me. "We hear reports that our youth leader is not teaching from the denomination's quarterly. Is that true?"

"Yes, it is true. I covered the mostly irrelevant material in one week, and lately we've been talking about the issues which are important to the kids."

"Well, that quarterly has served us well for many years. If you wish to continue, please go back to the lessons in the book."

I looked into the eyes of the pastor and his deacons and said, "I'm sorry. Those kids are too important for that. Please find another person to lead the music and poison the minds of your precious young people." And I walked away. As it turned out, that was just the first of several run-ins I would have through the years with church culture and tradition which left me extremely disillusioned. There seemed to be a huge disconnect between what I was learning in the Bible and what had evolved into "church" as it was conducted around me.

I graduated from LeTourneau College in May of 1968. God was gracious to enable me to receive my Bachelor of Science degree in Mechanical Engineering, Aeronautical Option with high honors. I immediately began looking for employment in the aerospace industry in the northeast as close to Boston as possible. While I waited on job offers, I stayed on campus and worked on my private pilot's license. Not long after my final check-ride with the FAA examiner (which I passed!), I walked into my dorm room and found an envelope on my desk containing something I had never seen before: a telegram. It was from a company called Itek Corporation. It said: "PLEASE COME TO LEXINGTON FOR INTERVIEW WITH ITEK STOP WILL PAY EXPENSES

STOP." I called the number immediately, and within a couple days I was being interviewed for my first job out of college.

6

Boston

I was hired on the spot. Engineers were in short supply in 1968. The Vietnam War was raging, and the so-called "military-defense-industrial complex" was booming to support the war effort with machines and weapons. And NASA was racing to fulfill President Kennedy's dream of putting a man on the moon before the end of the decade. The region around Boston was one of the major centers of engineering leadership for these efforts. Itek was a company which had sprung up as a military defense contractor to provide state-of-the-art cameras for the Air Force. The U-2 was flying secret spy missions at seventy thousand feet, particularly over the Soviet Union, and it carried a sophisticated Itek camera able to photograph objects as small as a chair from high altitude. Of course, I didn't know all that when I got hired because it was a top secret project.

I flew back to Longview, packed up my life into my Mustang, and headed for Boston. Cathy was thrilled I found a job close to her. She was beginning her third year at nursing school. I rented an apartment in Arlington and began work as a fledgling aerospace engineer.

The first couple months were pretty boring since I didn't have a security clearance. But once the clearance arrived, I was assigned to the thermal group of engineers who were redesigning the U-2 camera for use aboard the Apollo service module to photograph the back side of the moon (which earthlings never see since the moon rotates on its axis in perfect synchronicity with its orbit, causing us to always see the front side). It was exciting work which I could sink my teeth into. My task was to interface with the computer as we tweaked designs to modify the camera to operate in the environment of space with no air to cool its motors and lens. The computer in 1968 occupied a thirty by thirty foot room, took input via boxes full of punched cards, and spit out its results on reams of interconnected paper. I was writing code in FORTRAN, taking it to the key punch people, and then feeding huge cardboard boxes of cards into the computer. It was very fulfilling work. The camera worked as designed, and I was thrilled when the astronauts were able to bring back huge cassettes of film detailing the lunagraphy of the backside of the moon. What was particularly amazing about the Itek technology was their V-8 Analyzer which used mathematics and physics to translate the two dimensional photos of the moon into 3-D images. I was honored to have a tiny piece of history.

Cathy was busy completing her nurse's training. It was tough to find time off together, but we made the best of every moment we could. One incident stands out during those last days of our engagement. It was during the bleak winter of 1969 (an historically snowy year). I took her out for the evening. It was snowing hard, and we couldn't safely make it back across Boston to her dormitory, so I brought her back to my apartment which was close by. With God's help, up to that moment, we had been successfully keeping our pledge of chastity till marriage. The studio apartment had only one single bed, and it was a cold winter evening. I gave her the bed, and

I told her I would sleep on the floor. But I've never been able to sleep on a hard floor, and did I say it was a cold winter evening? So I climbed into bed with her. With clothes on, of course. At least we could keep each other warm. She was torn and I was torn. I started to pull her close to me, and she, praise God, shouted, "Ron, God doesn't want us to do this yet!"

I came to my senses, jumped away from the bed and spent the rest of the night on the cold, hard floor. God powerfully used Cathy to preserve our virginity that night, and it enabled us to prove our trustworthiness to each other which never dimmed throughout our forty-eight years of marriage.

We were married on June 14, 1969, just three months before Cathy graduated from nursing school. After an amazing honeymoon in Yosemite, we settled into a little one bedroom apartment in the Brighton district of Boston, very near where Cathy went to work as an RN after graduation. We were actively involved in the life of Ruggles Street Baptist Church where we were married. Shortly before our wedding, I was approached by the main deacon telling me that they would like to nominate me for the deacon board in the church election which was coming up soon. I told him, "I'm about to go on our honeymoon for two weeks. Cathy and I will pray about it, and I'll get back to you."

Of course, as Cathy and I talked and prayed about it, it was abundantly clear that I, at age twenty-two and just married, was in no way qualified to be in leadership of a church like that. But when I reported my decision to the head deacon, he said, "Sorry, we already held the election, and you were elected."

The experiences I had on that deacon board only served to further underscore the disparity I was seeing between the twentieth century western church and the first century church. For example, at my first meeting we were interviewing a pastoral candidate. He had done his homework and investigated the Roxbury neighborhood around the church building. In its heyday, Roxbury had been a thriving middle class borough of Boston, but now it had deteriorated into a predominantly poor neighborhood. It was the ghetto. But instead of developing a heart of loving compassion for the precious needy people around them, the members of Ruggles Street Church had all escaped from the slums and were now slipping back into the ghetto just long enough to attend services and leave again. Our candidate shared his loving heart and his vision to see us reach into the neighborhood with the love of Jesus. I got excited. Then one old deacon hunched his shoulders and barked: "If you're going to make us talk to *those* people, I will not support you." That laudable candidate did not become the pastor.

At another meeting, a strident argument broke out between two deacons over whether our church should have two pulpits (a smaller one on the side for the mere reading of the Bible and another larger one in the center for the preaching of the sermons) or just one multipurpose pulpit. In my youthful naïveté I couldn't believe men of God would fight over such things. I would come home to Cathy after every deacon meeting and ask, "How did the church migrate so far away from the simplicity of the early church as recorded in Acts?" All told, I lasted about three months on the deacon board and resigned.

Despite my disappointing experience on the deacon board, Cathy and I did have some very positive moments at Ruggles Street Church, particularly with the college-and-career-aged young adults. Boston is the hub of several major universities, and we had the privilege of connecting with about thirty bright, college-aged, committed followers of Jesus. For close to a year, I led our Sunday School class and began to experience the Holy Spirit exposing my nascent teaching gift to foster the discovery of scriptural truth. They were not like the men on the crusty deacon board. They were open and hungry to learn how to live out their faith. We opened our apartment to them and had sweet fellowship around Jesus. Between our involvement with the C&C group, and our full time jobs, we were pretty busy. We started to slip into the rut of getting so involved in the day-to-day activities of life and church attendance that our time with Jesus in His Word got subtly pushed aside. How easily we lose our focus on the important things.

One day in the fall of 1969 I received a phone call from a man named David Moreland. He had been my supervisor at Word of Life, and I liked him. He called himself a "hundred percenter." Today we would say he was "all in" for Jesus. He lived about an hour outside of Boston. He called to invite Cathy and me to join him and two other couples in a home-based weekly Bible study which he led. With characteristic Dave Moreland enthusiasm, he offered, "Ron, I know you and Cathy will enjoy this and greatly benefit from it!"

Well, I listened and then politely declined, explaining that we were quite busy with our active church and work lives. But David wouldn't take no. About ten days later he called again. Same proposal. Same polite dismissal. And again about a week later he called. By the third time I was more than a little annoyed. I wanted to say, "Dave, just leave us alone. We're fine without your Bible study." But for the sake of getting him off our backs, I acquiesced, "OK, we'll join you this week to check it out."

However, when I told Cathy, I said, "We'll go, and we'll politely tell them this doesn't work for us."

Praise God for Dave Moreland's persistence! He was obviously an anointed instrument through whom the Holy Spirit worked to ignite a flame in our spiritual growth. Cathy and I drove (on snowy New England back roads) to the home of the couple who was hosting the Bible study. Soon the group was sharing what they had studied that week. We were drawn in almost immediately. It was electrifying. The Spirit of God (who had spoken through a human instrument just days before) now started speaking to both of us *directly* saying, "This is what you need!"

We couldn't wait to get started. We joined the group, and it changed our lives. For the next five years (one in Boston, four in Santa Cruz), Cathy and I worked our way through a systematic study and life application of all the books of the New Testament, one chapter at a time. It laid a solid foundation in our lives just as Jesus promised it would in Matthew 7:24-25: "Therefore everyone who hears these words of mine and puts them into practice is like a wise man who built his house on the rock. The rain came down, the streams rose, and the winds blew and beat against that house; yet it did not fall, because it had its foundation on the rock" (NIV).

The Apollo space project was a smashing success. We put a man on the moon! And from *my* perspective we mapped the formerly unseen side of the moon. But once the goal was achieved, President Nixon and Congress slashed NASA's budget triggering massive layoffs in the aerospace industry. In the late winter of 1970, I received my pink slip and began seeking God to find out what He had next for me. Fortunately, Cathy was securely employed as a psychiatric nurse at St. Elizabeth's Hospital. Ruggles Church (the name changed when they bought a new building which wasn't located on Ruggles Street) employed me for a couple months on their building maintenance crew. There were other engineering jobs available, but I found my taste for big corporate employment declining. I was coming to terms with how God made me. I was more entrepreneurial. I was coming to appreciate being able to set my own daily schedule and leave time for people and things which mattered for the Kingdom of God.

Days before our wedding in June 1969, I had gotten my last haircut for a long time. Since childhood I had worn short hair—what is variously known as a crewcut or flat top or buzz. But after that wedding haircut, I started letting all my hair grow. A year later in the summer of 1970, I had longish hair and a full bushy black beard. The former clean-cut "geek" now looked like a hippie. I would tell critics (including my mother!), "God makes it grow, not me."

A ministry opportunity came to Boston sponsored by Intervarsity Christian Fellowship. They rented a house in Cambridge near Harvard Square and brought college kids from around the country to stay for the summer. The point was spiritual formation and outreach to the huge student population. Cathy and I joined the group and spent a lot of time at the Summer House encouraging the students as well as evangelizing on the Green of Harvard Square. On Cathy's days off, she would put flowers in her hair and play the tambourine (painted with a dove, of course). I would bind my hair with a handkerchief and play my 12-string guitar. And we would tell those who gathered about Jesus.

As I said, I was hired to help for a few weeks that summer on the renovation of the new Ruggles Church. They had given up on Roxbury and were moving to Brighton near our apartment. It was an expensive move, and the church leadership hired a company to come and solicit bonds from the membership to finance the purchase. When the solicitor arrived, he was invited to speak to the congregation and explain how he was going to be contacting everyone personally to pray with them about lending money for the project. In the course of his talk, he shared a very tender, tear-jerking testimony of how he had met Jesus personally, had his life transformed for Jesus, and decided to help God's people by financing their church buildings. A few days later my path crossed his in the church office. He was a friendly "salesman type" and began telling me about his busy schedule. His next stop was a Jewish synagogue, and then it was on to a Unitarian church. I furrowed my brow as I asked him, "How do those groups receive you as an evangelical follower of Christ?"

He smiled his broad salesman's smile and matter-of-factly said, "It's no problem. I have a Jewish testimony and a Unitarian testimony and a Catholic testimony, etc. I can bring tears to any group." I wanted to puke. The man was a shyster and a phony, a modern day Pharisee—the kind of person Jesus excoriated! Once again, I was confronted with a profound disconnect between what I was learning in the Bible about the beauty and simplicity of the early church and the ugliness of the way much of the modern church culture had evolved. I loved Jesus, but I wasn't sure I loved the church.

As the summer of 1970 wore on, I still had no clarity from God about what I should be doing with my life. Then, sometime in August my dad called from Santa Cruz: "Ron, the building business around here is booming. I can't keep up. I need a project foreman. Would you be interested in coming home and joining Kingham Construction? I will teach you what you need to know."

Cathy and I prayerfully considered the offer, and we both felt a clear leading from God to make the big move. It would open the door for more entrepreneurial freedom. I would be going home. But Cathy would be leaving everything she had ever known. She bravely reminded me she was my partner, and she wanted to be by my side wherever God sent us.

We made preparations to move across the country. A friend agreed to drive our rental truck so that we could take a road trip in the Mustang. We were confident Cathy would be able to find work as a nurse. We were finished with Summer House. So everything was buttoning up nicely except the ministry to the Ruggles Church college and career (C&C) people. God was using us there, and we hated to see it come to an end. We prayed, "Lord, who will take over for us?"

As we prayed, God put a couple into both of our hearts, Jim and Carol Schuttinga. So mere days before we pulled out of Boston, we invited the Schuttingas to join us for dinner at a downtown restaurant. We didn't tell them why. As we chatted over the dinner, I gently threw out how God had put their names on our hearts as we had prayed. Jim's eyes widened. "That's amazing!" he said. "We've felt a burden from God to ask *you* if we could step in and take over." Needless to say, we left Boston with hearts of eager anticipation, knowing that the God of answered prayer was going ahead of us. Again.

7

Santa Cruz—God's Call

After a memorable cross country road trip, we settled into a nice two-bedroom apartment in downtown Soquel, California. Cathy quickly found work as an RN at Community Hospital, and I began my apprenticeship as the construction superintendent of Kingham Construction. I rapidly learned the business, because for the first couple weeks Dad took me around with him to all the jobs and explained everything. He was a veteran builder and developer, and I absorbed his wisdom and experience. Of course, a huge part of the joy was the mere fact it was my dad, my hero. We talked as freely about the Lord as we did about six penny ring shank flooring nails.

An example of this blessing happened during those early weeks. We went to check on a house which was in the frame stage, and the roofers were busily nailing down shingles. In 1970 there were no compressor-driven nail guns. The roofers still used roofers' shingling jacks—a narrow hybrid of a hammer and a hatchet. Just as Dad and I approached the house, one of the roofers swung his jack, and it went flying out of his hand landing twenty-five feet from the house. He let out an exasperated holler, "God damn this job!"

Dad calmly went over and picked up the flying jack and carried it up the ladder to the disgruntled roofer. As he handed it to him, he lovingly said, "I'd appreciate it if you didn't ask

God to damn this job. I asked God in prayer this morning to bless it." I never heard that roofer utter another curse word around my dad.

I learned to estimate and order lumber, materials, and concrete (never forgetting that a cubic yard is twenty-seven cubit feet...) and coordinate with the labor crews and subcontractors. I drove around in a pickup with a lumber rack to make my rounds of the jobs. At the busiest of my four years in Santa Cruz, we had about twenty projects going at once. Dad was in his mid-fifties, and as I became more proficient in running the jobs, he and Mom started taking more time off for vacations. Because of Dad's impeccable reputation for integrity and quality, Kingham Construction stayed busy.

After about a year in the apartment, Cathy found a sleeper-lot on Hardin Way on the hill above Soquel. We were able to buy it with the money we had saved from Cathy's employment. When she went to work for Community Hospital, we had agreed she would save her entire paycheck (less what belonged to the Lord, of course). Since we now owned the lot free and clear, a local bank was happy to lend us what we needed to build the house. Cathy and I had the fun of designing, building, decorating, and furnishing our first home together. My crews and subs gave me special deals, so we were able to enjoy that spacious home for a payment of $135 per month. It was a two-level, four-bedroom-two-bath with 4"x12" open beams in the ceiling. When the fog would clear, it had an inspiring view of the Los Padres Mountains across the blue waters of Monterey Bay. We could have happily stayed there for a long time.

As we settled into life in Santa Cruz, we joined Twin Lakes Baptist Church, my home church growing up. We quickly made friends (it was amazing how quickly Cathy bonded with all these strange Californians!), and we became part of a large group of young couples called the Homebuilders. They had a regular Sunday morning class and periodic social gatherings. At times we would find great joy and profit in our gatherings at TLBC, but at other times we would experience that same puzzling disconnect I experienced in Longview and Boston.

Before our wedding, Cathy and I had prayerfully decided to wait about two years to have children. So not long after we got settled in Santa Cruz, we agreed it was time to "burn the diaphragm" (the method we had chosen for birth control). Cathy, being the nurse and astute student of human anatomy and physiology that she was, had chosen that method because it did not mess with the woman's hormones (like the pill) and did not abort a fertilized egg (like an IUD). So we had a little ceremony and asked the Lord for children. Cathy was ready to be a mom! As each month went by, she would be heartbroken when her monthly flow would appear. After three months we consulted with our doctor, Dr. Seapy. He was a family friend who actually still made visits to his sick-at-home patients. Cathy checked out fine. But lab tests revealed I had a very low sperm count. The doc gave us the word that we only had a one in a million chance of having a baby! We wept long and hard together. We had set our hearts on being parents, and it was a blow to think we were infertile. We asked God to miraculously intervene on our behalf, and at the same time we began to talk about how God might use us as a childless couple. Or perhaps we could adopt. Then one day Cathy said, "Ron, I just remembered a talk I heard from a gynecologist in nursing school. He said that a man's sperm is very fragile and dependent on the temperature of his groin. He added that he had seen a man simply change his underwear from jockeys to boxers and cool the testes just enough to boost the sperm count. Why don't you try boxers?" Well, I never liked boxers. Too floppy, if you get my drift. But I said it was worth a try.

Well, within two months Cathy reported nausea as she woke up one morning. She scurried to perform the pregnancy test, and the rest is history. Our first child was on the way. More tears—only this time they were tears of joy. How many people do you know who have two complete sets of underwear for birth control? This little trick worked for us for the next five years until—for some reason known only to God—I became quite potent while wearing jockeys and Cathy conceived identical twins!

God created Cathy to be a mom. Even in the yuckiest moments of a difficult pregnancy, she would giggle and say, "I'm going to have a baby!" She embraced her divine calling, pursuing excellence with joy and enthusiasm. She read profusely about childbirth and motherhood. One day she said, "Ron, I want to deliver our baby with natural childbirth."

I had no idea what she was talking about. So she gave me some materials to read. Natural childbirth via "Lamaze" was the trendy new thing in the early 1970s. What had been the norm for childbirth for millennia was suddenly novel all over again. For several decades in America mothers had been drugged so heavily that they had no memories of the labor and delivery. Cathy wanted to be wide awake and not drugged during the delivery, and she wanted me to be her coach. There was an introductory Lamaze class coming up soon, and she wanted me to check out the movie.

I said flatly, "No way. I'll pray for you in the waiting room while the doctor and nurses deliver the baby. I can't handle the sight of blood."

But she kept after me. So finally on a warm September evening (the only time it ever gets warm in Santa Cruz) she dragged me to the meeting. The upstairs room had no air conditioning, and the room was stuffy and close. It was filled with pregnant ladies with bellies protruding emitting heat in a way only late term pregnant ladies can do. People kept coming in until it was standing room only. Just before they started the movie, a *very* pregnant lady came into the crowded room. Being the gentleman I was, I stood up and gave her my seat. So they rolled the movie with me standing up against the wall.

Soon it was graphically displaying a woman giving birth. I got *seriously* queasy; my heart started racing; and I was about to faint. The woman to whom I had given my seat saw me tottering, and jumping up, she gave me back my seat! I made it through the movie, but that incident convinced me I could never stand in the delivery room as Cathy's coach.

However, praise God, Cathy was persistent! She wanted her baby's father to witness its entrance into the world. So I agreed to do it because I loved her, fully expecting to disappoint her. I remember crying out to God, "Please help me not faint in the delivery room." Well, when the big day finally arrived, God stepped in and powerfully overcame my weakness about medical procedures and blood. It was a sweet delight to pray with Cathy and coach her through the stages of labor *contractions* (Lamaze teachers did not allow us to use the word *pain*). And then I had the thrill of witnessing our son Nathan Ronald poke his little head out into the big wide world! It was the most beautiful thing I had ever seen. Instead of fainting, I shouted for joy when Nathan appeared, and I even laughed when Dr. Seapy got a little over anxious to deliver the placenta, and dropped it on the floor, splattering blood all over everything in the delivery room! By the way, Dr. Seapy was the one who had told us we only had one in a million chance of ever having a baby.

I was aspiring to be a man of God, and He knew that that included overcoming my squeamish cowardice about blood. God used Cathy's persistence to help me tap into His abundant flow of transforming grace. I was blessed to help with the birth of all five of the children God gave us. What an unparalleled experience it is to see a little person enter this world! And that certainly wasn't the last time Cathy's gentle persistence would have a powerful impact on the reshaping of this aspiring man-of-God-in-the-rough.

As soon as Nathan arrived, Cathy pushed the pause button on her nursing career. We both felt quite strongly that she had a divinely ordained role to play as a full-time mom. She engaged in her calling with her whole heart, and it paid eternal dividends in the shaping of our children's lives. She never left our home for work again until our youngest were in Junior High. Cathy truly loved her role as Mom, and God richly blessed her efforts.

I mentioned that we were attending the Homebuilders Group at church. It was being taught by a dear man named Bill Claypool. He had been appointed by the church leaders. He was back in the U.S. after having invested a chunk of his life with Wycliffe Bible Translators overseas. He loved Jesus and was a truly faithful saint. But as a teacher he was about as engaging as a soggy firecracker. It was hard to sit through his classes. Cathy and I observed that our group of bright and strategic young couples were slowly being desensitized to the explosive power of the gospel. We talked and prayed fervently about what we should do. We didn't want to hurt dear Bill Claypool, but we wanted to see the group come alive for God. After a gripping time of prayer, Cathy and I became convinced that God wanted *me* to take over teaching the class! Humanly speaking, this seemed totally wrong. It appeared arrogant and selfish; it was outside the accepted channels for appointing teachers at that church; and the students were my own peers! But the experience with turning over the class to the Schuttingas in Boston, just a couple years before, gave us a precedent that perhaps this truly was God's doing.

So with Cathy on her knees in prayer, I dialed Bill Claypool on the phone. After the normal pleasantries, I got to the point: "Bill, I know this sounds arrogant, but we sense God wants me to take over teaching your class. Would you be willing to pray about it?"

His answer bowled me over! "Ron, your call is an answer to *my* prayer. I've been painfully aware I am not gifted as a teacher, and I care about those wonderful young couples. I would love to have you assume the teaching role. My wife and I will continue as sponsors."

I was amazed. We had indeed heard the voice of God, and He was speaking to Bill *at the same time*. I immediately began teaching, and God used me to challenge those young couples with the message of the Word of God for the last two years we were in Santa Cruz. He also used that experience to expose me to more flaws in my own character as well as some of the hazards of ministering in the name of Jesus. I'll explain shortly.

In the late summer of 1971, I witnessed another rather dramatic and miraculous answer to prayer. Dad and I had not gone backpacking together for a few years, and we got the itch. So we carefully planned a week's adventure of fishing in the alpine lakes of the Trinity Alps in northern California. We left early one August morning from Santa Cruz and drove to the trailhead outside Trinity Center. It was about noon as we gathered our gear and got ready to lock up our truck for the week. If you've ever backpacked, you know every ounce matters. We carefully reviewed the contents of our packs and even our pockets. Dad pulled out his little leather change purse and said, "We certainly won't need any money while we're out, so I'll leave this here." It went into the truck, and we locked it up and headed out on the trail.

It took the rest of the afternoon to ascend the slope of a steep ridge above us. Once we got to the top, we started looking for a suitable campsite. We bedded down in a beautiful grove of trees near a gushing spring. It was idyllic. The Trinity Alps do not draw the same crowds as we were used to in Yosemite. That first day we never saw another soul on the trail. The solitude was precious. Both of us absolutely loved being out with God in the midst of His grandeur.

Next morning we broke camp and began working our way south along the ridge. By mid-afternoon we spotted our destination, two pristine lakes situated below the west side of the ridge. We had been on the trail for two days now, and we still hadn't seen another hiker. Our hearts soared with anticipation about the first bite on our fishing lines. Suddenly Dad grabbed his chest as though he was having a heart attack and announced, "My hearing aid batteries are dead." We stopped hiking, and he began to pound his pockets for the change purse where he always kept his spare batteries. "It's in the truck," he whimpered disgustedly.

We took off our packs, sat down, and began to assess our situation. Dad was now completely deaf. That meant he could talk with me, but I had to gesture back to him. As we peered at our gorgeous destination below us, we "talked" about our possibilities. There seemed to be only two rather discouraging options: spend the rest of our trip with Dad unable to hear anything I said, or turn around and get the batteries in the truck. The latter option would mean we would lose most of our week just getting back to where we were. It was very discouraging. So we prayed. Dad had no idea what I said, but I heard his heart pour out his confidence that God was good, and that He would show us what to do.

As we finished praying, I felt the old engineer surge within me. What did we have, and what did we need? I gestured to Dad to show me the batteries in his hearing aid. They were about the diameter of AAA batteries but half the length. We determined their voltage was very close to the AA batteries in the one tiny flashlight we carried. We quickly agreed we could do without the use of our flashlight at night as a tradeoff for his hearing. Then we assessed the contents of our packs. We had a couple "twisters" for the plastic bags we brought to carry out fish. They contained tiny wires (which we hoped were electrically conductive). And our first aid kit had tape. Now Dad was energized. He set about making a little external battery pack and taped the wires to the dead batteries in their little battery compartment. Bingo! He was on the air!

We burst out in loud praise and thanksgiving for God's wisdom and provision of just the right supplies and the knowledge to figure out a solution. We were in the middle of repacking our packs when we heard voices coming up the trail. They were the very first people we had seen since we left the day before! We had to tell them about our wonderful answer to prayer. When Dad finished enthusiastically telling them the story, one of the men asked us, "What kind of flashlight do you have?"

We showed him. It was exactly the same as his! He offered, "We're on our way out. Would you like my batteries?" That little Rube Goldberg battery pack lasted the whole week, and we had light after dark to boot. We didn't catch many fish on that trip, but we surely caught a glimpse of the loving care of our Heavenly Father. Thirty years later when I was going through my dad's things after he passed away, I found that little battery pack in his jewelry box on the top of his bedroom dresser. He had saved it all those years as a quiet monument to God's faithfulness in answering our prayer.

Around this time, Pastor Kraft reached out to about eight of us young men in the Homebuilders Group. He said he would like to appoint us to what he dubbed the "Young Men's Advisory Council" (YMAC). He wanted his older leaders to hear some fresh thinking about how we should "do" church. To put it lightly, we young bucks jumped at the chance! We were thrilled to be given this important opportunity to perhaps steer the church more in the direction of the early church. We met together for several weeks, praying and discussing at length the things we felt were essential to Jesus' plan for His church. We also talked about the cultural things which, like barnacles, had accreted themselves to the hull of our ship, getting in the way of Jesus' plan. The group appointed me to be the spokesman. Pastor Kraft set a date for our presentation to the deacon board. I prepared a fifteen-minute report which was illustrated with a flip chart on an easel.

The day came for our report, and most of the men of the YMAC gathered outside the door of the meeting room to pray while I went in and made my presentation. I was about midway through my talk when an older gentlemen suddenly broke in, directing his words to Pastor Kraft: "Who *is* this young man? What is this group he represents?" (Remember, I had grown up in that church and been very visible, including being the teacher of the Homebuilders Group.)

The deacons began buzzing in agitation, and so the pastor asked me to step outside. My buddies were eager to hear how it went. I told them I didn't think it went very well. Moments later, Pastor Kraft came out and announced, "I'm sorry, men. They disbanded your group."

In hindsight, I see what happened. They had expected us to offer novel ways to make the church more relevant, not more Biblical. Our questions and suggestions were an assault on their traditions, so they killed the messenger rather than listening to the message. Once again, I found myself in a very frustrating place. I was deeply in love with Jesus and His plan for the church, and yet I was losing faith in the way modern-day church was being conducted.

I was quite pessimistic, actually. My disappointment with the church often slipped out in discussions with friends. Thus it was extremely significant (in God's providence) that our church featured a guest speaker one Sunday at about this time named Dr. Vernon Grounds. I don't remember much of what his sermon was about, but I will never forget a statement he made that found its way into my heart like an arrow. At the time, I thought the quote was original to him, but I later learned that it could be traced as far back as Confucius. Dr. Grounds spoke about the way many followers of Jesus were loudly decrying the evil conditions of the world at that time. But he believed that such negative outcries only served to polarize and exacerbate things. Rather, he believed God wanted us to take little positive steps of love in the name of Jesus. He said, "You can curse the darkness or you can light a candle." That notion resonated deeply with me. I couldn't cure all the ills of the church, but I could (as the old gospel song says) let my little light shine.

I was indeed seeing good fruit teaching the Homebuilders Group—my light was shining there. Cathy and I were constantly blessed by our weekly personal Bible study with two other young couples. I was finding joy in meeting with men in personal discipleship—my light was shining there also. We started a group called the Friday Family. We made a covenant with four couples who came to our home for dinner every Friday night. We ate, prayed, sang, took the Lord's Table, and read the Word together. Everything that involved homes and small groups was a blessing—and my light was shining there. But it was the big church in the big building that was such a great disappointment.

One day we were expressing our disappointment and confusion to a friend named Terry Chappell. He and Marilyn were part of our Friday Family. They had recently moved to Santa Cruz from Palo Alto. He told us we should pay a visit to Peninsula Bible Church some Sunday evening. He said they were having success trying to recapture the dynamic of early church "body life." The pastor had even written a book about it. So we took him up on it.

A few weeks later, my parents watched Nathan while we drove "over the hill" to visit Peninsula Bible Church. Pastor Ray Stedman was leading the body life service. It was held in a huge auditorium inside an old Safeway building. There must have been a thousand or more people packed in like sardines. I had never seen anything like it. In my experience, church had always been conducted from the stage while the audience passively watched from the seats. But in that service a man with a wireless microphone was running around and passing the mic to the people in the seats as they raised their hands to share. Some were sharing scriptures which encouraged or challenged them. Others shared answers to prayer. Some recounted experiences leading someone to Jesus that week. Some stood and offered a word of exhortation. Others shared burdens which someone else would offer to pray for. It was riveting. It was like a big small group. But the moment that is emblazoned on my memory was when a man stood up, took the mic, and began telling us how he had been ministering to a man in the county jail for several months. He had led him to Christ. Now his time was served and he was being released the next morning. He was planning to pick him up, but his car broke down today, and could we please pray that someone would pick him up. He sat down. Instantly a voice from way across that huge crowd shouted out (without the mic!), "It's a white Chevy, license plate such and such." And he hurled the car keys to the man who shared the burden. I welled up with tears. *This* was what I had read about in Acts. It was indeed possible to do church like Acts in a big building in the twentieth century! That experience fueled my growing desire to see the church restored to the beauty, power and simplicity of its roots. I found myself daily grappling with how I would fit into that picture. How could I light my candle instead of cursing the darkness?

One Sunday morning in the early summer of 1973, in the midst of my soul-searching, Pastor Kraft was absent, so the sermon was delivered by one of his underlings named Roger Moore. Roger was not an eloquent speaker, but he *was* a dear man of God who loved Jesus and His Word. He had the audience turn to 1 Corinthians 12, and he began presenting his message about the importance of each Christian knowing and then serving Jesus within his/her unique giftedness. I knew the passage well from my own personal Bible study. He did a good job talking about the wide variety of gifts which the Holy Spirit has given to His people. He started working with Paul's analogy—the human body. Each member is unique and vital. Then he leaned into the pulpit, eyes seemingly on me, and said, "Some of you are gifted by God to be an invisible, behind the scenes, liver, but you are pridefully trying to function as hands. And some of you are just the opposite. You are gifted by God as hands, hands of public leadership, but you are shyly hiding as a behind-the-scenes liver. Confess your pride, accept the way God made you, and by faith step into your giftedness."

Roger went on for another twenty minutes, but I never heard another word He said. I tuned exclusively into the Holy Spirit and started acknowledging that I was indeed a hand. I had seen God use me as a leader and a teacher. I recognized my shepherd's heart and my passion to see the early church culture re-established. I heard God's voice clearly calling me to step away from the business world and focus my entire life encouraging and teaching His flock. I had seen it work at the church I visited in Palo Alto. I knew Jesus was alive in me. So I presented myself to Him to do with me as He desired. But I knew I needed to be equipped. I would need training in how to communicate God's word from the original languages (Greek and Hebrew), and that typically happens in schools called seminaries. Over lunch that day, with Nathan munching his vittles in the high chair next to us, I tearfully shared it all with my precious mate. Cathy listened with rapt attention, and then she said, "I knew this was coming a year ago, Ron. I wondered how long it would take for you to finally hear God. Let's do this together!" What an amazing partner God gave me.

But then it struck me: *"How can I leave Kingham Construction right now? Business is booming, and my sudden departure would certainly throw Dad into a serious depression."* (He had previously suffered two year-long bouts with debilitating depression.) As much as I was ready to pack up and move away right then, we realized we should give Dad a year's notice, and then we would head off to seminary. When he got our news he was thrilled. He appreciated the one-year's notice, but he was especially excited to see me heading for "the ministry." Then he told me something I never knew. He said that when I was born, he had dedicated me to God and asked God to call me into the ministry. He never wanted to influence me by telling me that, but now that it was clear God was calling me, he told me. Wow! It is an uncanny feeling to realize you are the embodiment of the answer to your father's long-ago prayer.

The next Sunday I shared my "call" with the Homebuilders. They were mostly affirmative, with a fairly notable exception about which I will share in a moment. In fact, one of the women in the class made a special trip out to our home in Soquel while we were eating lunch to deliver a message from the Lord to me. She stood outside our front door and said, "Ron, I just want to confirm your call. You are truly gifted by God. When you are teaching, I hear God talking to me." What a beautiful endorsement that God was at work in me! This business of learning to discern the voice of God is pretty tricky, especially when the future of your family is at stake. To have unsolicited corroboration at that moment was *huge* to me.

So the next year was all about winding down my work at Kingham Construction and ramping up my plan to train for the ministry. My first step was to enroll in the beginner's Greek class at Bethany Bible College in Scotts Valley. I would squeeze the one-hour classes into my daily schedule of moving about the construction sites. As I had been learning the scriptures over the past four or five years, I had repeatedly bumped into interpretive questions which were difficult to resolve without a working knowledge of the original languages. I had longed to learn Greek, and now I had the chance. I think I was one of Dr. Ryder's favorite students because I was so eager to learn. When we began class we had two books to buy: a grammar text and the Greek New Testament. I remember opening the Greek New Testament and thinking it looked like a chicken had stepped in some ink and walked all over the pages. The first semester was entirely devoted to working with the textbook, learning to read the Greek letters, and memorizing vocabulary and verb paradigms. Finally, as we began the second semester, Dr. Ryder told us to open our Greek New Testaments to 1 John 1. He said John's writings were the simplest Greek, and we should be able to read it now. I can still remember it like it was yesterday: I opened my Greek text and began reading what John had written—not what translators told me he meant. I read *his own words*—and understood them! O my! I sat at my desk and quietly wept for joy. Having first year Greek under my belt gave me a marvelous running start when I finally hit seminary that next fall.

During that year of transition, God continued the crucial process of burning away character traits in me that didn't match Jesus' character (a process, by the way, which is still underway, of course, as I write these words!). When I made the decision to leave the construction business and attend seminary, as I've said, the business was booming. But very soon afterwards, a serious retraction in the economy stalled new building, and I found more time to actually work with my hands on the jobs instead of overseeing the crews. One day I was in the middle of building a fence, and a small convertible sports car pulled up to the job. Out jumped Greg, a young man in my Homebuilders Group. "Hey, Ron, got a minute to chat?"

"Sure," I said, as I dropped my tool belt and sat down on a pile of lumber with him.

After a few words of light chit chat, he got down to business. "Ron, I need to share something with you since you are sensing God's leading about going into the ministry. Do you see the neighbor's lawn over there? I can think of at least two ways to cut that lawn. Push a lawn mower over it, and it will look neat and trim and start growing back again. Or you could bring a big bulldozer into the yard and scrape the grass off. It will certainly cut the grass, but the grass might never grow back again." He paused, carefully put his finger on my chest and added, "Ron, you're a bulldozer." Then Greg quietly climbed back into his car and drove off.

I sat there for quite a while trying to figure out what had just happened. Could Greg be correct? Was I a bulldozer? Or was he just a messenger from Satan trying to dissuade me from following God? When I went home that night, I shared the incident with Cathy, and we asked God about it. Lovingly, the Holy Spirit confirmed Greg's prophetic words to me. He showed me a frightfully glaring weakness in my character which did not allow me to be sympathetic to other people's struggles. I expected others to "buck it up" and move at my pace. I realized I needed to enroll in the Spirit's school of compassion. I could never be a shepherd to God's sheep as a bulldozer. So it was that I embarked on a life-long education of learning to feel what others feel, especially the people I love. I certainly haven't attained to the level of the compassion of my Lord yet, but praise God, I'm not the bulldozer I was in my twenties. Thank you, Greg. You courageously delivered God's message to me.

It was also during this year of transition that God wisely introduced me to the hazards of being a leader in His kingdom. One Sunday evening after church service, we were invited to join four other young couples for pie and coffee. Cathy and I thought it was just for informal chit chat and fellowship, but apparently, it was a set-up. They were wanting to talk with me about my teaching. As we sat in a circle around the living room, one of them started off with, "Ron, we've been wanting to share some thoughts with you about Homebuilders Group."

I said, "Great."

And then they started in. As I reflect back on it, I'm reminded of the staccato dialog in the Broadway Musical *The Music Man,* which goes, "Pick a little, talk a little, pick a little, talk a little, cheep cheep cheep, talk a lot, pick a little more…." They began to systematically barrage me with all the reasons why they did not appreciate my teaching in the class. At one point, Cathy nudged me and whispered, "What are you going to say?"

I just shook my head. I did not know what to say. At some point, the negativity died down, the subject matter changed, and we were finally able to say goodbye and escape home. I had taken a huge gut punch, and I had not said anything more than, "Wow…. OK…. Oh…, etc."

Cathy and I immediately began to pray about what this meant: "Lord, help! Am I the wrong guy for the class? Should I resign? Am I not a gifted and called teacher? Have I done something wrong for which I need to apologize?"

We decided to wait for God's answer during the week and address the matter as He directed us the following Sunday in the class. In our small group personal Bible study that week we were working on 2 Corinthians. In that book, Paul writes with great love, compassion, and commitment to his beloved spiritual brothers and sisters in Corinth even though they didn't always like him. For example, he quotes his critics in 10:10: "They say, 'His letters are weighty and strong, but his personal presence is unimpressive, and his speech contemptible" (NASB). But he goes on to say he is confident

God commended him to that ministry, and he would not stop bringing God's Word to them.

I asked the Lord several times that week whether He had truly called me to teach that class, and every time I asked I sensed His encouragement to press on and not quit. Then towards the end of the week, I read an article in *Christianity Today* which was an interview with Billy Graham. The great evangelist was asked about his response to one of his loudest critics named Bob Jones who at that time was publically raking Billy over the coals. Graham simply answered, "I don't answer to Mr. Jones. God called me to this ministry, and I answer to Him."

That was the final word I needed from God. I would not say anything to the class on Sunday and simply press on in our continued study of how to live out the meaning of Jesus' amazing Sermon on the Mount. I remember it as a wonderful class: great discussion, meaningful application, and honest grappling with the truth. And for the weeks which followed, I continued to love and teach the group, and they responded marvelously.

About a month after the "Pick a little" pie gathering, the man responsible pulled me aside after class. He said, "Ron, I want to apologize to you on behalf of all the couples who tore you apart a few weeks ago. God has shown us what was going on. You are our contemporary, and yet your spiritual progress is outpacing ours. We felt ashamed. It was easier for us to try and knock you down than to be inspired by your example and grow along with you. Forgive us. We are excited for your future in ministry."

What an amazing experience that was! I am so grateful God taught me to *expect* flack and critics. That lesson would stand me in very good stead in the years which were to follow.

When critics come at us, we must listen to them carefully and then ask the Lord to shine His light upon what they have alleged. If the light reveals sin or weakness in us, we must allow the prophetic criticism to correct us (like the bulldozer incident). But if the light vindicates us, we must press on. Satan will always be trying to derail our progress.

Now, the question of where I would study began to loom large. I gathered catalogs from ten seminaries. I quickly eliminated most of them because I was seeking training in the original languages as well as communication skills, and most seminaries only gave a polite nod to Greek and Hebrew. All but one required three years to graduate. Only one actually focused on the Biblical languages and required four years, and that was Dallas Theological Seminary (DTS). I knew of the school from my brief exposure to Dr. Howard Hendricks at Word of Life eight years earlier, but I really had no idea if it would be a good fit for me. Before I actually applied, I wanted to make sure it was right for me. Having grown up in Scotts Valley, I was quite familiar with Mt. Hermon Christian Conference Center nearby. DTS has held a week of meetings at Mt. Hermon since time immemorial, so I checked their schedule. It turned out that Dr. Hendricks was one of the featured speakers in the summer of 1973. So I decided to drive up to Mt. Hermon and listen to his morning message and then see if I could grab him for five minutes afterwards.

That morning, Cathy and I did what we had been doing for the last four years. We had a separate Quiet Time with the Lord in His Word and then spent a few minutes together sharing what He had shown us. My Quiet Time was in Psalm 90, and the verse which grabbed me was, "So teach us to number our days, that we may apply our hearts unto wisdom" (v. 12, KJV). Cathy's QT was in Isaiah that day, and the verse which stuck out to her was, "And He shall be the stability of your times, a wealth of salvation, wisdom and knowledge…" (33:6, NASB). We were astounded by the way God had spoken to us both about the importance of our time. I kissed her goodbye, and asked her to pray for me as I tried to connect with Dr. Hendricks. I drove to the conference center, and the meeting was already in progress, so I sat out in the open patio behind the old auditorium. Dr. Hendricks took his place at the pulpit and began, "I'd like you to turn with me to our text this morning, Psalm 90. We're going to talk about the importance of the way we invest the time God gives us."

I almost fell into the shrubbery. I was in a decisive search for how Cathy and I were to invest the next several years of our lives, and God was getting my attention. I successfully grabbed Dr. Hendricks after the meeting, asked him for a few moments, drove home to Soquel, got Cathy, hustled back, and together, we spent a wonderful fifteen minute interview with him. I asked him simply, "What is DTS trying to accomplish with its graduates?"

His answer was exactly what I was hoping to hear: "We're equipping men to know the Word with confidence so they can live it themselves and then proclaim it with clarity and persuasive power to God's people." That was how I wanted to invest the next four years of my life, so I went home and started applying to DTS. In God's grace, I was accepted to enroll in the fall of 1974. I remember the sobering acceptance letter from Dr. John Walvoord, the president. He welcomed me to the seminary, and then pointed out that three men had applied for every available seat. I had better take my place seriously.

Sometime in the fall of 1973, I changed underwear, and Cathy found out she was pregnant. So while I was learning Greek, teaching class on Sundays, preparing my mind to become a student at DTS, and supervising construction projects, she was anticipating our second child and preparing herself to be a pastor's wife. The construction business had been drying up during my last year with Dad, and my approaching departure provided him the impetus to simply close down the company and retire out of town. Cathy and I had just settled nicely into our home on the hill looking out over Monterey Bay, and now we were planning to pack it all up, sell much of the life we had accumulated, and move to Dallas. It was an exciting time, and yet a time of great sobering awareness of the road which lay ahead for me, especially as I would be stepping into leadership in Jesus' church—a church which I was very conflicted about. But I was absolutely certain God was sending me. God was obviously talking to other people about us as well. Over the last few months before we left for Dallas, no less than four families came to us (without our ever asking!) and said God told them to send us money every month while we were in seminary.

Four weeks before our scheduled departure date, little Jonathan Edward made his appearance. The second time around we were veterans, and the delivery went perfectly. Dr. Seapy didn't even drop the placenta! We gave him the middle name Edward because he was born on my dad's birthday! And as the years went by we were astounded by the many ways Jon resembled his grandpa. How does God do that sort of thing?

Shortly after Jonathan was born, God graciously enabled us to sell our home and carry back paper which would provide us a regular monthly check while in seminary. Between the four individuals who were giving, and the note income, we were promised a regular income of more than $400 per month. We anticipated a monthly budget of somewhere around $700 per month (it was the early '70s...), so I was only going to need to earn $200 or $300 a month while I studied. God was certainly paving the road to seminary.

For the first time in my life, I was about to step out in faith in a way that involved serious risk. I was going to take my young family to a place where we didn't even know a single soul. We were going to need housing. I was going to need work to support my family. I was going to need wisdom and strength to balance family, work, and rigorous graduate studies while Cathy stayed home and cared for our children. We were leaving behind an excellent job with a solid income and entrepreneurial freedom, a brand new house with a breathtaking view, a doctor who still made house calls, and family and longtime friends. I had no idea how any of this was going to work. From a human standpoint, it made absolutely no sense. But from the stories I have shared in this chapter, I had direct, irrefutable evidence God was calling me. I needed to obey. But I was anxious. Was I crazy? Only days before our time to leave Soquel, I remember sitting out on the cantilevered deck of our house taking in the view with Nathan on my lap. I peered into his precious face and said, "Son, we're going to stake our lives on this promise," and then I opened my Bible to a passage I had been discussing with my Homebuilders Group and read it out loud:

> "Do not be worried about your life, as to what you will eat or what you will drink; nor for your body, as to what you will put on. Is not life more than food, and the body more than clothing? Look at the birds of the air, that they do not sow, nor reap nor gather into barns, and yet your heavenly Father feeds them. Are you not worth much more than they? And who of you by being worried can add a single hour to his life? And why are you worried about clothing? Observe how the lilies of

the field grow; they do not toil nor do they spin, yet I say to you that not even Solomon in all his glory clothed himself like one of these. But if God so clothes the grass of the field, which is alive today and tomorrow is thrown into the furnace, will He not much more clothe you? You of little faith! Do not worry then, saying, 'What will we eat?' or 'What will we drink?' or 'What will we wear for clothing?' For the Gentiles eagerly seek all these things; for your heavenly Father knows that you need all these things. But seek first His kingdom and His righteousness, and all these things will be added to you. So do not worry about tomorrow; for tomorrow will care for itself. Each day has enough trouble of its own" (Matthew 6:25-34, NASB).

Then I shouted towards the sky, "Lord, I'm seeking Your kingdom. Now You come through!"

So the first week of August 1974, we hired a moving company to pack up our earthly goods into a huge moving van. It started the long, ten-day road trip to a yet-to-be-specified address somewhere in or near Dallas, Texas. And we said farewell to our family, took baby Jonathan and two-and-a-half-year-old Nathan in our arms, and stepped aboard a plane for Dallas. Our hearts were soaring with the thrill of adventure....

8

Dallas—Equipping the Servant

The sign on the door said "Admissions." I tentatively approached the counter. I was on the campus of Dallas Seminary. I had exchanged a lot of paperwork with this office, and so it was my natural port of entry. Cathy and the boys were holding out in the motel room we had rented after we arrived the day before. A perky young woman (I still remember her name: Jean Diffenderfer...) came bustling up to meet me and jubilantly exclaimed, "Welcome to DTS, Mr. Kingham. Do you prefer to be called Ron or Ronald?"

It was like the voice of an angel speaking from heaven. You could have knocked me over with a feather. "Well, thank you. But how did you ever know my name?" I queried. She explained that there was a photo on my application, and she had made it her personal project to memorize all the new students' faces (some three hundred!) before they ever arrived. She wanted to help us all feel a warm welcome as we began our seminary experience. I was truly amazed. I found out a few weeks later as classes began that some of my professors also did the same thing. They could face a hundred new students in a lecture hall and call them by name the first week of classes. This early red-carpet welcome became emblematic of my four years at DTS. It truly was the place where I belonged, and I thanked God every day for the joy and privilege of being there.

That experience also burned a passion into my heart for my life ahead as a shepherd of God's flock: Know your people by name! I learned that everyone bears an invisible message which reads, "Please validate my personal worth and individuality by calling me by my name."

We had arrived about four weeks before classes began so we could get settled and be ready to roll once school began. God was gracious to help us. The seminary assigned us a "big brother and sister"—a third year student and his wife (Larry and Kathy Walker) who gave us temporary free housing in a vacant unfurnished apartment they managed. They were so helpful to these newbies! We bought a brand new Dodge Mitsubishi microvan for which we had set aside money before we left Santa Cruz. We followed Larry and Kathy's recommendation to search for housing in the eastern suburbs of Dallas. We felt pressure because the moving van was in transit, but we also knew how important this house would be for the next four years. I remember sitting on the floor of that vacant apartment in prayer asking God to show us where to live. Cathy found a friendly realtor with a good-ole-boy Texas accent and attitude to show us available properties in Mesquite, the eastern suburb which seemed affordable. We absolutely loved a little 1,000 square-foot brick two-bedroom-one-bath on a corner near the ramp leading to Interstate 20. We were ready with cash for the down payment (from the sale of the house in Soquel), but we needed a monthly payment that would fit our Spartan student budget. We were used to California real estate prices. Cathy and I were ready to make an offer. It was raining as we sat in the car outside the cute house and asked the realtor, "So how much are they asking for this place?"

"Ninety-three," he said. "Is that too much for you?"

We had just sold a much more valuable house in Santa Cruz for $135,000. We were hoping to downsize significantly for our stint in seminary. "Yes, it's a little high," we responded. "We're trying to keep our monthly payments very low while I go to seminary."

There was a long pause, and then our realtor friend said, "Maybe we ain't communicatin' here. What I just quoted you is *the monthly payment*. This house is selling for $27,000 and has an assumable loan at $93 per month which includes your taxes and insurance."

Bingo! We bought the house. And the escrow closed so quickly we even had time to do some painting before the moving van arrived.

By the time classes began at school, I had remodeled the kitchen cabinets and counters and partitioned off a portion of the dining area into a study for me. It was a large corner lot with open space across the street. I put up a swing set, built a sand box for my sons (which the neighborhood cats also found quite attractive...), and we were settled in for the next four years. Just weeks before, I had emphatically told the Lord I was trusting Him to "come through" on His promise to care for us, and we were living in the midst of the first clear evidence He was indeed coming through.

Seminary was an absolute joy! I was surrounded by men and women of God who took their faith seriously and knew and loved God's Word. The professors, with only a couple exceptions, were brilliant, engaging scholars who lived what they taught. On the other hand, many of my classmates were twenty-two year-olds, straight out of university, with little or no experience in "real" life and/or ministry. I, of course, had been out of college and engaged in life for several years. I could often feel the difference in how we approached the subject matter, especially in the theology classes. They were often fascinated with solving the unsolvable questions like the proverbial "How many angels can dance on the head of a pin?" or debating the arcane distinctions between infralapsarianism and supralapsarianism. In contrast, I evaded those questions while I asked, "How will I use this information with God's people in the future?" But there were many students like me, hungry to be equipped as servant-leaders in Jesus' kingdom. Of course my primary objective was to learn the content of the scriptures and the various tools and study techniques to carry on a lifetime of in-depth study. By the time I graduated, I had indeed received thorough training in the languages (three full years of Greek exegesis and two full years of Hebrew exegesis); I was thoroughly trained in how to ask and find answers to interpretive questions; I had built a library of tools (books, mostly) which would help me find answers to those questions; and I had been equipped with methods of communicating God's truth which I could employ to convey the Word to God's precious flock. It was all I could expect, and more.

Speaking of communication methods, the seminary completely tricked me into learning one of the most valuable tools I garnered while at DTS. It was one of my last semesters, and I was choosing electives in my major, Pastoral Ministries. The course description of the class called Effective Pulpit Delivery said something bland like, "This class will equip pastors to bring life and freshness to their preaching."

"*That sounds helpful*," I thought. So I enrolled.

On the first day of class, the professor spilled the beans. He confessed, "If I told you what we were *really* going to do in this class, you wouldn't have signed up, so I tricked you. I'm going to teach you how to be actors and put drama into your sermons." All of us students (especially the geeky engineer types like me) gasped. We were trapped. But I look back with great gratitude for what Dr. John Reed taught us stiff academics. He loosened us up and taught us the rudiments of how to use our bodies and voices to tell stories like Jesus did. For the final in that class I wrote, memorized, costumed-up, and then performed a monologue of the story of Elijah. Dramatic sermons became one of the most anticipated tools in my communication toolbox in the twenty-four years I ministered in Woodland. And in the process, Elijah became one of my personal heroes.

One of the ironies of my training at DTS is that some of the personal theological views I have come to hold in later years (particularly eschatology and pneumatology) are not in agreement with the official doctrinal position of the school, yet I arrived at my views using the methods of Biblical exegesis and interpretation which I learned *at DTS*. In essence they taught me how to disagree with them!

Cathy was amazing during our years in seminary. We shared one car, our little Mitsubishi microvan. Whenever I had the car at school or work, she was at home with the kids. She never felt trapped there, but rather she worked hard to make the home a place of fun and learning. She was constantly teaching the kids. Nathan learned to read at about four-and-a-half, and by the time he started kindergarten in the fall of '77, he was reading full length "chapter books." I remember the day we went to kindergarten orientation. We politely told the teacher to expect Nate to be a reader. She politely responded back in her winsome Texas drawl, "Well, Y'all, lots of parents think their kids can read because they see the golden arches and say, 'It says, McDonald's.'"

We just smiled. A few days after school started, Nathan reported she had made him a teacher's assistant. She would have him take three or four kids to a corner and read stories to them while she worked with the other kids! It was because of Cathy's unswerving determination to be the mom God called her to be.

Larry and Kathy (our big bro and sis) invited us to visit their church our first Sunday in Dallas. It was pastored by a man named Gene Getz who was attempting to revitalize church life in Dallas with body life much like Ray Stedman was doing in Palo Alto. Cathy and I were sold the first week. The church, Fellowship Bible Church, was located about forty minutes from our house in Mesquite, so we were thrilled to learn that they were just about to launch a daughter church in Garland (ten minutes from Mesquite). We helped establish Garland Bible Fellowship, and served there for our tenure in Dallas. Cathy and I teamed up to teach children for about a year, and then I moved on to serving in various forms of leadership, joining the elder team and ultimately being ordained just a couple weeks before we left Dallas to move to Woodland. GBF gave me hope. It showed me it was possible to address the problems I had encountered in my previous church experiences.

We had saved up enough money before we went to Dallas to carry our family for about three months without my going to work. That was a good move, because it enabled us to establish some new routines in our new town with just one car and with me going to graduate school. When it was time to find work, I prayerfully wrote out a little 3x5 card which said simply, "Ron Kingham, Home Repairs, call ___," and thumbtacked it to the bulletin board in the student café at the seminary. Within a few days I received the call I mentioned when writing about my first job to replace the leach field at my home in Scotts Valley. I happily dug up and replaced the sewer lateral for the man who called me. And somehow (well I actually do know how: God keeps His extravagant promises to provide) from that day onward, I never lacked work as a handyman. Just when I would need to close our budget gap with a few hundred dollars, the phone would ring and I would have a job. People would usually begin their phone call with, "I was talking with so-and-so. They told me you did work for them, and they recommend you." Word of mouth became my sole form of advertising. My life became a billboard for the truth of Proverbs 22:1: "A good name is to be more desired than great wealth; favor is better than silver and gold" (NASB). Towards the end, I was too busy and had to turn jobs down. In subsequent years I have told countless friends and mentees how important it is to maintain a good reputation for reliability, good craftsmanship, and dependability. I remember one customer who hired me after she had run off three other people because one wouldn't do what she wanted, the next wouldn't show up when he said he would, and the third got drunk in the middle of the job.

My financial diary from seminary days is a testimony to God's creative providence. No two months of income were alike, but our needs were *always* met. My favorite story illustrating the amazing ways God provided for us during those years is the time I was hired to remodel a laundry room in the home of a couple in a nice neighborhood in North Dallas. Both of them worked (I didn't know where), so they met me one evening to show me what they wanted and then gave me a key to the house. It was a job involving moving a partition, some plumbing, and then sheetrock with a smooth finish. They wanted to do the painting themselves. So I set about to do the work on my days off from school. I never saw them once while I was there. The job was almost complete. All that was left was the twenty minutes of final sanding of the wallboard and vacuuming up the dust.

It was a school day. I was about to leave Cathy and the boys, and as I kissed her goodbye, she said, "Try to come straight home from school because we're completely out of food, and I need to go shopping this afternoon." Then she stopped, got pensive for a moment, and added, "Never mind. There's no money for groceries in our bank account."

I said, "Well, I'll come straight home after I sand that job. It'll only take me an hour or so." Then I left for school. When classes were over, I buzzed out to the job in North Dallas, did the sanding, cleaned up, and was in the process of filling out my job invoice for them to mail me a payment. I would have been gone in about another minute. But suddenly I heard the door open. At first I thought it was a stranger because my customer, the owner, had long hair and a bushy black beard. This man had short hair and was clean shaven. But when he spoke I recognized him. He said, "Hi. Looks like you're about done."

I said, "Yep, I just finished." Then I told him I didn't recognize him at first.

He said, "I just came from the barber. I quit my job. I couldn't tell you this before, but I was an undercover detective for the Dallas Police, and I have been breaking up drug rings. My name is out there, and I couldn't take it anymore, so I quit. Your work looks great. Would you like a check now?"

I said, "Sure, Thanks." So he wrote me a check, and I drove home to Mesquite as quickly as I could.

Cathy greeted me at the door, and then she sighed, "There was no need to rush. No one sent us any money in the mail today." Remember, we had four dear friends sending us support money each month.

114

I reached into my pocket and showed her the check and said, "God caused a cop to quit his job *today* so we could have money for food."

We truly lived by faith during those years in Dallas. To this day I am still blessed and amazed I graduated from four years of graduate school debt free. God enabled us to have just what we needed *every* step of the way. Mere days before the beginning of my fourth year, I had no idea where I was going to get the money to enroll. Then I received a surprise letter from a bank in town. It said a man had died and left an endowment for young men pursuing the gospel ministry. They had selected me as the recipient of a $1,000 scholarship. Praise God! That was just what I needed to register for classes. Each time one of these experiences would happen, I would think back to the day on the deck in Soquel with son Nathan on my lap telling God I was going to trust Him and He'd better come through. And I would also go back further to the day in my dorm room in Longview when I told the Lord I needed evidence He was alive and well in my life today. I learned a lot in Dallas. Much of it wasn't in the classroom. I know it's written in the Book, but I learned it in the hard knocks of life: God is an incredibly good God who keeps His promises.

Many of those hard knocks revealed parts of me that were not at all Christlike. One of the items that needed some attention was my academic pride. Sometime in the spring of 1976, Cathy announced she was carrying another baby. We were thrilled. Maybe the Lord would send us a girl this time. Thankfully, the pregnancy was not as hard as the first two, and she was able to keep up with her responsibilities quite well despite my busyness at school and periodic work. We started thinking about names for both a boy and a girl (this was prior to ultrasound). I can't remember the boy's name, but I do remember the girl's name because God did indeed grace us with a gorgeous daughter in January 1977. We chose Bethany. I was by now (at least in my own prideful mind) both a Greek and a Hebrew scholar. I knew from the New Testament that Jesus loved to hang out in Bethany with His dear friends Mary, Martha, and Lazarus. So the name was special to Jesus. And from my "excellent" knowledge of Old Testament Hebrew, I was sure the underlying name came from the Hebrew "Beth" (*house*) and "ani" (first person suffix, *my*). What a beautiful name for our beautiful daughter, "My House." So she arrived, and we sent out the birth announcement to our friends and family. I got a call from my sister back in California. She said, "Ron, I know how careful you have been to name your kids with Biblical names which have significant meaning, so I looked up Bethany in my Bible dictionary. Maybe my book is wrong, but it says the name means "house of affliction or house of figs."

I was puzzled. So I looked it up (which I had never done—I only went by my excellent knowledge of Hebrew). Sure enough, Judy was right. I placed a handle on my daughter based on my *excellent* knowledge of Hebrew which wasn't so excellent after all. A little knowledge of Hebrew or Greek can be a dangerous thing. I felt quite chagrinned. Thank God, that little gaffe knocked me down several notches in my pride. And it has made me extremely wary ever since. Before I ever explain any Biblical word or concept, I carefully do my homework. Thank God for my sister's gentle love. And thank God, sweet daughter Bethany has risen above my foolishness.

Another aspect of my character which God started addressing during my years in Dallas was my anger. He knew that sinful anger would do damage to the work He was calling me to, namely that of a servant-leader in His kingdom. The problem was, I didn't believe I had an anger problem. I never screamed or threw things. I never cut loose with a string of filthy swear words. So my anger—though very present and observable by those close to me, especially Cathy—was off my personal radar. The first warning flag went up early in my seminary journey. A seminar was offered to train people in the use of the Taylor-Johnson Temperament Analysis. I knew it would be helpful for me to have that certification, especially in marriage and pre-marital counseling. So I took the seminar and was certified. As part of the training, Cathy and I took the assessment on ourselves. Cathy's chart looked just like I knew her: emotionally mature and balanced in every way. Mine however, showed the expected scores for a visionary leader with one serious blemish: I scored extremely high in hostility. I can remember telling Cathy that the TJTA must be flawed. I just knew I didn't have that kind of hostility in me. She said something like, "Well, maybe you should ask the Lord about it." But of course, since I knew the test was flawed, there was no reason to ask the Lord about it.

Then sweet Bethany arrived into our household in the cold winter of '77. It was the semester I was enrolled in Hebrew Exegesis of the Psalms—one of the most academically challenging classes at DTS. Our precious little one was a colicky baby, and she would wake up at night screaming in obvious digestive pain. Cathy and I would take turns getting up with her and try to settle her down and get her back to sleep. One night it was my turn. I got up with her and tried to soothe her with everything I knew how to do—but to no avail. She kept shrieking in pain. I walked her. I spoke gently to her. I hugged her tightly to help her feel secure. No change. And then I snapped. I grabbed her by the neck and started choking her to make her stop screaming. Praise God, I suddenly awoke from my momentary psychotic state and realized what I was doing! I quickly carried my precious baby into the bedroom, woke up Cathy, handed Bethany to her, and said, "I almost killed our daughter."

I was shaken to the core.

I slipped into my study and got on my knees and confessed the horribleness of what I had just done. I prayed the prayer of Psalm 139:23-24 which includes these words, "Search me, O God, and know my heart; try me and know my anxious thoughts; and see if there be any hurtful way in me, and lead me in the everlasting way" (NASB). And the Lord started showing me my anger. It was connected back to the incident at Westmont; it was connected to my present pressure to do well in my Hebrew Exegesis class; and it was all about my personal plans and goals being thwarted by others getting in my way. I was staring into the abyss of my sinful anger. I truly confessed it that night, but I didn't fully grasp how much my propensity to anger could damage my future ministry until another year went by. I did not see that it was anything more than an isolated aberration. Satan had blinded me to interpret my anger as part of the fabric of my personality. But that would change.

One of the final hoops I was required to jump through in order to graduate was a personal counseling session with Dr. Paul Meier. It was mere weeks before graduation. Prior to the session he had me take the MMPI (an upgraded personality testing instrument which can only be administered by licensed psychiatrists and psychologists). It's highly regarded as an extremely accurate measure of human personality. Cathy and I sat down in his office, and he began to discuss the results of my test. "Ron, your profile looks really encouraging. You are a born leader and visionary. You are self-disciplined and won't need others to prod you. I think God can use you very significantly in His kingdom." I felt great joy. I smiled. I was on the right path. "But, Ron," he continued solemnly, "I'm *very* concerned about your score on the hostility scale. You're filled with defensiveness and passive aggression. It can sabotage all you do both in your family and in the church. You must face it and ask God to root it out of you."

Needless to say, this was the topic of our conversation as Cathy and I drove home that day. I asked her, "Do you regularly see anger in me?"

She just nodded.

I said, "Sweetheart, please pray for me. I need to ask the Holy Spirit to change me." And at that moment I committed myself to a personal growth project (which continues to this *very* day) to see God transform my prideful and angry actions and words into Christ-like gentleness and compassion. I am so grateful for the experiences God orchestrated at DTS to expose this ugly weakness. I truly was in denial.

You see, change requires an honest willingness to quit rationalizing our anger—or any other sinful weakness. Up until that point, I actually believed that my angry actions were an emotional knee-jerk for which I wasn't responsible. One of the first lessons God taught me, once I was acknowledging my anger, was that I actually delighted in it—it soothed my hurt ego. I asked Cathy to let me know whenever she spotted anger in me, and I promised to face it. Then I learned to ask God to show me why I am angry (which He is always ready to do!). The next step is to confess whatever sin God shows me. And finally, I learned to ask the Holy Spirit to replace my hurtful attitude with the gentle character of Christ. More than forty years later I can joyfully report that the vast part of my angry temperament has been replaced by the sweet fruit of God's Holy Spirit. I am so grateful to God for teaching me how my anger was in an unholy partnership with my ugly, selfish pride.

I also had lessons to learn about my lack of empathy, sensitivity, and compassion (remember the bulldozer...). My mister-fix-it mentality doesn't mesh well with the pain and problems most people face. One Sunday I was the designated sharing leader for the body life service at Garland Bible Fellowship. I did not personally know many of the people who were present. Someone shared about a young father named Bill with three young children who just lost his young wife to cancer. He worked nights at the post office, and was struggling to figure out what to do with his kids. Would the church please pray? I looked around the large group and said, "Who would like to pray that this dear young man finds a new wife?"

I'm ashamed to even remember that I could be so insensitive. But in my mister-fix-it mentality, I honestly couldn't think of a better way for God to solve His need. Well, someone prayed for the hurting young man, but not for a new wife. When the service was over, one of the other elders came over to me and said, "You'd better go speak with Bill. He was here, and he's devastated."

I asked someone to point him out to me, and I walked up to him. I felt awful. He looked at me and said, "You obviously didn't know my precious Mary, did you?" The dear guy was in the depths of grief, and I had run over him like a bulldozer. On the way home that day, I wept as I told Cathy my desperate need to learn to feel other people's pain.

Not long after that Sunday, I had another opportunity for God to drive that lesson home to me. For a class in Field Education, I was assigned to an eight-hour shift at Parkland General Hospital alongside the chaplain to learn about hospital visitation. I was only there for about an hour when he was suddenly called away to the emergency room. After instructing me to cover for him, he sent me to the aid of a woman who was sitting in the surgery waiting room. She had just received word that her mother's cancer was inoperable. I had never done anything like this in my life. As I was finding my way to the waiting room, I asked God, "What do I say?" But I heard nothing.

I entered the room, identified myself and sat down next to her. I asked her what happened, and through halting tears, she told me. I sat in silence, tears starting to leak from my eyes. I kept thinking, "*What do I say?*" Nothing came, so I sat for probably fifteen minutes in silence, wiping tears, thinking about what I would feel if she were my own mother.

Finally, I stood up, said I needed to meet the chaplain, and left the room. I found him with the family in the ER, and after another hour or so, he said, "Let's go back and see the woman you visited."

As we entered the surgery waiting room, the woman looked up, and said, "Oh, thank you, Chaplain. There's the young man who was *so* helpful to me." I gasped inside. I had said absolutely nothing to her. I didn't even pray. But then the truth dawned upon me: people in grief need our presence and tears, not our words. Scores of times in the subsequent years of my ministry I revisited that lesson learned at Parkland Hospital.

I mentioned in Chapter One that I started out life with a great loathing of vomit. Well, by the time I finished my years in Dallas, God had helped me completely grow out of that aversion. A rather humorous story happened midway through our Dallas years which illustrated the growth God was working in me. Three pregnancies and three little kids had forced me to take puke in stride. One night when Jonathan was about three, he called out in the middle of the night, "Daddy, I feel sick."

So I leapt out of bed and ran for the kitchen in the dark to fetch a pot to collect the offering. The path in our little house from the master bedroom to the kitchen involved several quick turns, and in my haste, I missed one. I brutally stubbed my toe, and I stopped in the hallway to nurse my screaming toe, groaning, "Ow…!" In the meantime, Jonathan had decided to head for the bathroom. Well, just before he made it to the bathroom, he plowed into me. I was dancing there on one foot, holding my sore toe, and he let his cookies fly all over my foot and the carpet! I started to laugh, although I couldn't laugh too much, because my poor little guy was sick. I turned on the light and shifted into clean-up mode. But I saw God's humor in showing me I wasn't afraid of vomit anymore!

When Cathy and I left Santa Cruz for our new life at seminary, I made her a solemn pledge: I was not going to allow school to supplant my commitment to her and the family. I promised her I would do my studying either in the early mornings at home (since I was a morning person) or during the daytime at school. I promised her the evenings would be family time. And God graciously enabled me to keep that pledge all the way through school. In the evenings I was there to play with the kids, bathe them, read stories to them, etc. However, in my third year, this commitment to family collided with my pride. I've already mentioned Hebrew Exegesis of the Psalms as being the most academically rigorous class in the curriculum. It was challenging, but I was getting it. Typical homework assignments would take five to ten hours. Sometimes I simply didn't have that much time. I can still see one of my homework papers that was returned to me with big red "D" written on it by the professor who graded it. He had written these comments, "You were doing great till you stopped. Why did you stop?"

I remember talking to that piece of paper for quite a while. Since my earliest days in school, I was always an A student. I simply didn't accept D work. It was a matter of pride. But praise God, I was able to tell the paper, "I'm learning what I need in the class, but I made a pledge to my wife and my family, and I will not renege on that promise just to get an A. And I will not offer any rationale or excuse to the professor. I will be good with a D if that is what I get." In God's grace I did well on the final paper, and it brought my final score up to a C. But I carried that powerful lesson with me all the rest of my days when the demands of ministry would start conflicting with my family commitments.

I had a serious scare in the spring of 1977, my third year at DTS, when I almost lost the normal use of my left hand. I was playing catcher for our church softball team. It was a fun source of camaraderie and exercise. I was behind the plate, with a man on third base. The batter hit a grounder to the short stop, and the runner on third started for home. We had him. The short stop threw to me. I planted my foot on home base and held out my glove to the runner (he was about 250 pounds) as he slid into the plate feet first. I got him out, and he crushed the middle finger of my left hand. I remember the conference with the medical people in Baylor Hospital the next day after they had had a chance to examine the X-rays. The first knuckle was shattered into *twelve pieces*. "But," they reported, "It just so happens the best hand surgeon in the Southwest is on our staff."

So Dr. Peter Carter was called. He studied the X-rays and said, "Well, Ron, based on my experience, it's likely you're going to lose the normal use of your hand, but if you'd like, I'll operate and try to restore some of the movement of your fingers. I can't make any promises."

I said, "Let's go for it."

The next day I underwent surgery in which Dr. Carter deftly packed all the fragments together, surrounded it with a huge cast which went all the way to the elbow, and then hoped for the best. I went back to school and functioned with one hand till school was out. The day came for the cast to come off. The doctor X-rayed it again and said it looked like it was healing well. He handed me a little container of medical Silly Putty and said, "Carry this around with you and work it in the palm of your hand as much as you possibly can."

So I began working the putty. At that point I could form a loose fist and then open it about one inch (like when you make a letter C with your thumb and fingers). That summer we decided to drive back to Santa Cruz for a visit with family for a few days. I was driving somewhere in hot west Texas with the family all ensconced in the Mitsubishi microvan. I was working the putty as I drove. Dr. Carter had told me to squeeze as hard as I could and to open my fingers as far as I could. All at once my hand loudly cracked! Everyone heard it. Had I worked it too hard? Had I broken a bone? But there was no pain. Gently I started opening my fingers, and they went all the way! Instantly, my hand was fully healed! As I type these words, I am still amazed at the miracle God wrought on my behalf, partly through the skill of Dr. Carter, and partly through direct divine intervention. My hand has been completely normal ever since. What a gift!

My final year at DTS was focused on researching and writing my master's thesis. I was also honored to be selected to teach in the seminary Lay Institute, classes which were offered to the public in Dallas. My thesis was called

"Television, the Preschool Child, and the Christian Home." It was a compilation of secular research on the effects of TV on kids under six evaluated in light of God's plan in the Bible for families. Of course, I had had personal experience with the benefits of raising my own kids without TV, so I was admittedly a little biased. One of the evidences that most impacted me was a study of kittens. Kittens are known to be born blind because their eyes are not completely developed at birth. They remain blind for about ten days. Researchers took a litter of kittens, stitched their eyes shut at birth, and then removed the stitches after ten days. All the kittens remained blind for the rest of their lives. Their eyes were programmed by their creator to develop in the light—but only during that early phase of their life. I correlated that with the development of children which God designed to only happen during those earliest days. I encouraged parents to utilize those precious moments to maximize their personal teaching during those irreplaceable years and not allow TV to block, blunt, or controvert their input.

By God's sustaining grace, I graduated from Dallas Seminary on May 2, 1978. The goal I had set was achieved, and I was now ready for God's next step in our lives. The four years went rapidly. I grew a great deal academically. I was equipped in ministry skills. My faith was enlarged watching God supply every need. And God was doing a marvelous work in me of burning off the dross of my old prideful, insensitive, angry self. Cathy and I were excited about what was ahead. While I kept busy with my carpentry business, we daily asked God what He wanted us to do next. Garland Bible Fellowship offered us a position on their teaching staff, but we felt we wanted to move away from the Dallas area. The region around Dallas was flooded with gifted DTS grads. We wanted to get far enough away so people would respond to us because they saw Jesus in our lives, not a DTS sheepskin on our wall. The seminary placement office arranged for us to visit two little churches, one in east Texas and one in Oklahoma. But both times we felt like the problems were deeply ingrained, and we would be fighting an insurmountable mountain of cultural momentum. We would find ourselves cursing the darkness, and we wanted to light our candle. We hungered to find people who weren't very familiar with traditional church, who would respond to Jesus in a way which was closer to the pattern of first century believers. We slowly came to terms with the reality that this meant starting something brand new. So I informed the placement office I was available to partner up with someone who wanted to plant a church.

Meanwhile, Cathy had become pregnant sometime around the first of the year. This fourth pregnancy was different from the first three. She was gaining more weight and girth than previously, and she had almost no morning sickness. I just thought she was carrying a big boy, but she started having secret suspicions and dreams (although she didn't tell me then) that she might be carrying twins. She started to talk about it around the time school was out. She would say things like, "This baby sure seems to kick more than our previous kids."

So as we waited for God's direction for our next vocational step, Cathy grew larger, and I busied myself with my carpentry work. I was building an elaborate fence for a client in the Park Cities area of Dallas. I had just bought an old beat-up pickup truck for my work, so for the first time Cathy was able to go to her regularly scheduled OB/GYN progress checkups while I was at work. Ultrasound was just appearing in the medical world. It was still very rudimentary and crude, but Cathy's doctor had just acquired a brand new machine. So she drove herself to the doctor one day in mid-June for her progress checkup. She told the doc her premonitions that something was different about this pregnancy. He measured her and agreed she was bigger than expected. So he said, "Let's use the new machine and see what's going on."

A few minutes later, the nurse, who was moving the probe around Cathy's abdomen, smiled and announced, "I see two heads in there!"

In sweet vindication, Cathy exclaimed, "I knew it!"

The nurse went on, "And it appears at least one of them is a boy."

Cathy was so excited she called the house where I was working to gush the news. I rejoiced with her, while I also swallowed the lump in my throat. "God," I prayed, "This a huge new responsibility. Help us!" Thus began our incomparable adventure of being parents of twins!

Not many days after finding out our exciting news, I received a call from the seminary placement office. The placement director, Dr. Bob Salstrom, told me he had received a letter from a couple in Woodland, California, who were looking for a young pastor to help them plant a Bible church there. Was I interested?

I scrambled to find a map and see where Woodland was. I told him, "Yes, send me the letter, and I'll give them a call."

During my years in seminary, my parents had closed Kingham Construction and moved to a new home at Lake of the Pines, between Auburn and Grass Valley, California. Woodland was only an hour and a half away from my parents. Cathy and I had often talked about the value of being near my aging parents, both for their incomparable influence on our kids as well as our responsibility to care for them in their later years. We had never heard of Woodland, let alone visited there, so we had no idea what it might be like. But we were ready for whatever adventure God had in store for us. So I dialed the phone and called the young couple, Don and Mary Thomas, who had sent the letter to the seminary.

We exchanged pleasantries, and then I asked them what they were looking for. Don told me he was a former hippie who had found Jesus. He was now starting out as a fledgling attorney. He said they were looking for someone to help them start a stripped-down church which wasn't cluttered with church tradition but focused on Jesus and the Bible. I said I shared the same vision and mentioned my desire to plant a body life church. Then Don asked me to tell him a little about myself. So I started in about my amazing family: "Cathy is a committed stay-at-home mom, Nathan is six, Jon is almost four, Bethany is one-and-a-half, and Cathy is carrying twins which are due in September. We are soon to be a family of seven!" I will never forget the long pregnant pause on the phone. I thought we had lost our phone connection.

Then Don stammered, "Oh…. We were looking for a young couple without kids so the wife could work to support the husband while we started the church."

I replied, "Well, Don, if that's what you want, I'm not your man."

But Don was obviously listening to the Holy Spirit, and he went on, "This whole thing is a venture of faith, Ron, so, why don't we fly you out to look over Woodland and we'll pray about our shared visions, and see what God wants us to do."

So sometime in late June, I flew to Woodland for a three-day visit with the Thomases. They showed me around, and we spent hours getting to know each other. There were several tradition-bound churches there, but no stripped-down body life ministries. We talked and talked and prayed and prayed about our visions for ministry. Don had a heart and gift for evangelism and was a guy who could make things happen. Mary was a sweet servant. By the time my visit came to an end, we had agreed we would make a good team, and that despite my "handicap" of five little kids, if God was in it, He would raise up "Woodland Bible Church" (WBC). It would be a venture built on faith in the sure promise of Jesus: "...I will build My church, and the gates of Hades will not overpower it" (Matthew 16:18, NASB).

Back in Mesquite, Cathy and I prayed and talked about this incredible opportunity. It would provide us a place to make and disciple believers without the encumbrances of lifeless traditions. But were we fools to make such a drastic move to a strange place with no guaranteed job and with such a large family of little ones? Soon we'd be changing three sets of diapers and be busy beyond description with our little family. Would we even have time left to do the work involved in planting a church? How could we move two thousand miles with three in diapers? Our thoughts and prayers shifted daily as we wrestled with this monumental decision. It was mid-July. The twins were due in late September (but twins notoriously come early, and in our case they did). Don Thomas had told me that, as a faith step, he and Mary had been putting their financial giving into a savings account called Woodland Bible Church. They had saved up enough to provide me a two-month salary when I first arrived. Cathy and I were grappling with the most challenging faith step either of us had ever faced in our lives. At times the line between faith and foolishness is fuzzy. But the more we struggled, the more confident we became. We triumphantly encouraged each other, "God wants us to go, and He's going to provide our needs."

It was another moment like the one on the deck of the house in Soquel before heading off to seminary. Together we prayed, "Lord, we hear you calling us to Woodland. Many people are telling us we are foolish. But we are confident You will provide if we step out in faith. Please come through."

We knew we would never go if we waited until we had three in diapers. So we concluded we needed to leave immediately. We would love to have six weeks in Woodland before the twins were born. The Mesquite house was in very good condition since I had been regularly upgrading and maintaining it during our four years in seminary. So it just took a couple days to clean and paint, and it was ready for the market. At the same time I called my Dad and asked him to see if he could find us a house in Woodland to either rent or buy. I told him my requirements were for a house payment or rent of no more than $300 per month (it was 1978, and that wasn't unreasonable). God was working in both places! I placed a little ad in the classified section of the local newspaper for an open house on Saturday. Cathy baked a loaf of bread and made the house smell scrumptious, and people started arriving early in the morning. By eleven o'clock a family came who liked it and bought it! We drew up a contract and took it to the title company on Monday, and the deal closed before we left town! The new owners got their own loan, so that meant we received about $35,000 in cash for a down payment on a home in California. Meanwhile, back in Woodland, my Dad talked with Don Thomas and found out his secretary knew of a house which wasn't yet on the market but was for sale because of a divorce. It was only four years old and was a four-bedroom-two-bath on a corner lot in the new neighborhood on the south side of town. It "happened" to have an assumable loan, and the payments would be about $340 per month. I agreed that

that was workable, so we faxed a power of attorney to him, and he made an offer on the house at 1649 College St. (which we had never seen—this was before the internet…). The offer was accepted, and we had a place to land—all in the space of about a week! I've been around real estate deals much of my life, and I've never seen deals move so quickly on both ends. God certainly was knocking down the roadblocks in the path of our new church-planting adventure. A wonderful footnote to this story is that a few weeks after we got settled into our new home, we received a letter from our new lender informing us that since the landmark Proposition 13 was taking effect, they were adjusting our monthly payment down to $298 per month!

We knew the airlines did not sanction passengers who were very pregnant (for fear they might go into labor on the plane), so the moment we knew our home sold in Mesquite, we booked an immediate flight for Cathy, Jonathan and Bethany. Let me reiterate, Cathy was *very* pregnant. She walked leaning backwards to keep from falling forward. Praise God, they let her on the plane, and my parents took her (and Jon and Beth) in for a few days. I kept Nathan with me in Texas. I finalized details of closing down our home in Mesquite, packed a rental truck, and hitched the Mitsubishi to trail behind. And after selling my old pickup to my next door neighbor hours before we left, Nate and I ventured off for a three-day father-son road trip across the hot, dry southwest in the first week of August 1978.

Exactly four years after we showed our faces in Dallas we were saying goodbye. It had been a momentous time of growth and change. God was busy shaping this servant. It was a time of being equipped and "de-quipped," as I have shared. It was a time of experiencing many amazing encounters with the miraculous grace of God. It had been thirteen years since I had placed my life in the hands of Jesus (at LeTourneau) asking Him to prove to me that He was alive and well and active in my life. There were no longer any questions about *Him*. He was alive and incredibly active! The questions which remained were about *my faith* in Him. Would I trust Him to enable me to weather the storms ahead for a new-fangled expression of the body of Christ in Woodland, California?

9

Really? That's Not How it's Supposed to be Done

I thought I had gone from the frying pan into the fire. What a greeting! As Nathan and I drove down the main street of Woodland in that un-air-conditioned Ryder rental truck, the huge thermometer outside the savings and loan read 118°. Nate's coloring crayons had been melting as he tried to work in his coloring books. This Santa Cruz boy had had some serious adjusting when I moved to Texas. *"But really, Lord? This is brutal. I don't want to live here!"* As it turns out, that was the hottest day I ever spent in Woodland during our twenty-four years there. I think the Lord was testing me. But I also am inclined to think it was a metaphor for what was happening on a more spiritual plane. God was about to do some wonderful work in pulling together the rudiments of a new church, but the trials would get hot. Would I run from the heat?

When I became convinced I was going to plant a new church, I realized I didn't know how to do that! Every church I ever knew about was already in motion. I had never witnessed a church start-up. One day in my last semester at DTS, I saw a notice for a brown bag luncheon on "How to Plant a Church." I thought, *"Great! Right up my alley."*

So I brought my lunch and listened as the leader talked his way through his handout of "The Twelve Proven Steps for a Successful Church Plant." I remember one of them was, "Wait until you have twelve committed families giving a tithe of their income before you go public and announce your grand opening." The whole thing seemed to me to be an adaptation of the way a person starts a business. God was hardly mentioned, and faith was absolutely absent. It was about proven human methods. So I was not drawn to that approach at all. When it was over, I went up to the presenter and asked him what church he had planted. He matter-of-factly said, "Oh, I have never planted a church. These methods are gleaned from those who have planted successful big churches."

I smiled, turned, wadded up the notes, and deposited them in the trash as I left the room. If God was going to start a church through me, it would have to have signs of miraculous intervention with the fingerprints of the Holy Spirit all over it. I wanted it to be His church, not my personal ego venture.

So now I was in Woodland, ready to plant a church. Where does one start? Of course the first matter of business was to reunite with my family and start moving into our new home. As I pulled up to the house, I sized it up and tried to decide if I liked this house my dad had found for us. It was right on the corner of College and El Dorado Streets, two obviously well-traveled thoroughfares through the southern end of town. On the corner south of the house was a huge open field filled with piles of dirt with dust driven by the south wind blowing right at the place. Cars were whizzing by the intersection on College St. because there were only stop signs on El Dorado Street. I had a bunch of little kids. I wondered if Dad had made a mistake. But we pressed forward. Inside, the house was quite adequate to our needs. Dad brought Cathy and the kids down from Auburn, and he and a neighbor helped me unload our furniture, and we began our new life.

Within a very short time, I would come to understand the incredible wisdom of God which was displayed in the purchase of that home on that corner! The field with the piles of dirt was actually a wonderful park which was just about to be developed. It made our little yard much bigger! And the visibility of our hard-to-miss big family with a bunch of little kids on that busy corner was priceless. I would meet new people in town, and they would say, "Oh, you're that family who lives on the corner. I've seen you out with your kids." Visibility was essential in planting a church, and visibility we had!

There were the normal move-in projects like installing a window in the master bedroom so we could look out at the new park from our room. We enrolled Nathan in first grade at the Woodland Christian School (WCS), and Cathy started familiarizing herself with the milieu of her new hometown. We started meeting almost daily with Don and Mary for prayer, asking God for His strategy. We decided to hold a worship, teaching, and sharing service in our new home on Sunday mornings. We had two of Don and Mary's friends join us on a couple occasions, but mostly it was just the Kinghams and the Thomases. That lasted for about two months. By early October Don had secured the old Women's Clubhouse on Lincoln Ave, and we announced our presence to the community.

Don and I had numerous meetings in those early days. We would pray and seek God's guidance and wisdom for this crazy venture of starting a brand new church. We discussed at length the many positive and negative qualities we had seen in our previous experiences. We searched the scriptures to find the essential traits that defined the early church. I remember drawing up a long list of items, and then scratching most of them off as "non-essentials." We boiled them down to three things which we dubbed "non-negotiables": (1) led by godly elders, (2) committed to the centrality of Jesus Christ and the scriptures, and (3) animated by the active work of the Holy Spirit in cultivating vibrant *koinonia* and body life. All other forms, activities, styles, traditions, groups, service formats, dogmas, etc. could come and go as dictated by the culture of Woodland, California, in the late 1970s. The church culture would spring from the culture of its people, not the other way around. In retrospect, I see now why people who were with us for a while and then had to move away would tell me there was no church like WBC anywhere else. It was intentionally unique.

Of course, the most pressing matter in late August and early September was when would Cathy deliver the twins. At times it was hard for me to resist chuckling as I watched her move about. For the last two months of that pregnancy, she basically waddled everywhere she went. We found a local OB/GYN doctor, and she started weekly checkups. I remember the evening we attended the birthing orientation at Woodland Memorial Hospital (WMH). This was our fourth hospital, and at all of the first three, the presenters had routinely said, "If you're having twins, the second one is free. You only pay for one baby."

Suddenly, this was relevant! Since we had no insurance, we had saved what we needed to pay out of pocket for one birth. The two-fer was going to be a great blessing. But the presenter at WMH made no mention of it. So I raised my hand and asked about it. "Oh, no," she said, "You pay for both births." Well, this provided us yet another opportunity to see God's hand of provision. He touched a dear friend to offer to pay for the second kid.

So it was that Peter John and Andrew David Kingham entered this wide world on the evening of September 11, 1978, ten minutes apart. In the delivery room, the doctor informed me he thought they were identical (even though one was a full pound heavier than the other) because they were both sharing the same placenta. But it would require an expensive lab test to prove it. We never got the test done, but our personal observations very quickly concurred with the doc. They truly were identical. What an amazing gift from God! Of course, I wanted to keep their little wrist bands on them permanently—or at least until I became convinced I could tell them apart. But it wasn't necessary. God graciously endowed Andrew with a little patch of blond hair in the middle of his dark hair for a birth mark. The presence of that mark was truly a blessing, because it was so important to me to know and love each son uniquely. That became a real challenge through their years of growing up. Most other people (with a few important exceptions) couldn't tell them apart. Throughout their school years, their pals and teachers would frequently simply call them Kingham. Identical twins have a mystical dynamic, in that they are emotionally connected in ways other siblings never experience. Cathy and I would watch them interact and simply marvel. Peter and Andrew did not have a personal language which sometimes occurs with identicals, but they did have a dual-think that transcended logic or rationality—like the time they were about five years old and were walking to meet each other at the park across from our house. As they approached they were singing the same song—at the same place in the song! Many times, Cathy and I told God how grateful we were to be the parents of twins. My challenge as a dad was to know how to affirm their duality while at the same time treat them as individuals. Sometimes I didn't do it as well as I would have liked.

Needless to say, our house was a very active place. Three in diapers! We had used cloth diapers (the kind with diaper pins) which Cathy washed at home for all the first three kids. Almost immediately after the twins were born, I saw that the best gift I could give my sweetheart was diaper service. Once a week, the Tidy Didee man pulled up to our house and collected huge bags of dirty diapers (we did rinse them out!) and replaced them with fresh smelling, fluffy, clean diapers, hundreds of them. She thanked me *many* times! I think Tidy Didee went the way of the slide rule when paper diapers came into vogue. God answered Cathy's prayerful desire that she be able to nurse both twins. So the formerly large bellied pregnant lady morphed into the voluptuous—milk for two—mama of twins. Most of the time she nursed them one at a time so she could nurture the mama-son connection with them individually. But one of my favorite memories is seeing her, when occasionally necessary, breastfeeding both twins at once. It was a worshipful moment for me. To see God pouring His provision and love for them through Cathy was indescribably beautiful. My mom came down and helped for the first week after we brought the twins home from the hospital, but after that we were on our own.

The reality of our situation seemed bleak. Perhaps Don's original idea of finding a man with no kids and a wife for financial support would have been better. Cathy was home with all these little kids in a new community without the support network of ladies from an established church. I was spending a lot of my time helping her with the kids. I had about a month more of the salary Don was giving us, and then I was going to have to find work. People had told us we were crazy

138

to test God like this. But I had learned a few things about the life of faith. One of the first principles is to be confident you know what God wants you to do. We had strongly felt His call away from the traditional American-style church, and we had seen remarkable provision as we made the quick exit from Dallas. We were confident God had sent us here! So I got alone with God and cried out, "Show me how to plant a church, Lord. Our family needs the support of the Christian community as much as anybody! Give us some people."

One of the things I had done almost immediately after arriving in Woodland was to scope out which churches in town might be threatened by the existence of non-traditional Woodland Bible Church. There were about seven, as I recall. I personally paid a visit to the pastors of each of those churches, introduced myself, and told them what I was doing. I said to each one, "I do not want to take any people from your church. If anyone slips away, I promise to send them back."

So Cathy and I could not build personal connections with any of the people from other churches, or else it would have nullified my pledge to the other pastors. We were there to build relationships with people who were without a church affiliation.

One day as I was prayerfully pondering the huge question of how to find the people who would form the beginning core of our new church, the Lord freshly brought to mind the words of Jesus recorded in Matthew 16:18: "…I will build My church, and the gates of Hades will not overpower it" (NASB). Suddenly I realized it wasn't my responsibility to build the church; it was His! He would do it. This took a huge load off my shoulders! So what, then, was my part? I was to be actively teaching the truth of God's Word (as per my personal gifting from the Holy Spirit, and which I was doing on Sunday mornings with the Thomases) and loving the people whom I contacted around me. Then the Spirit impressed me with the challenge of James 1:27. I saw that the people I should be looking for were the very needy. It says, "Religion that God our Father accepts as pure and faultless is this: to look after orphans and widows in their distress and to keep oneself from being polluted by the world" (NIV). So I prayed, "Lord Jesus, please bring us someone in serious need whom we can love in Your name. I will study and teach whomever you bring to us, and I will wait and watch while You build Your church."

We saw God answer that prayer in just a matter of days! Cathy met Mary, a young single woman in town with three very small fatherless children. Her family had just rescued her from a dreadful cult in Central America where she had been terribly abused by the cult leader. She was lost and bewildered and showed signs of demonization. She truly was needy! We surrounded her with love, and God started healing her. We brought her groceries, baby-sat her kids, helped with her rent, cut her boys' hair, and even bought her a little car. And she started fellowshipping with our little group. I remember the red letter day when we had a marathon prayer time as God drove the demons from her mind.

At the same time, God started bringing people to us. We would meet them around town, and God would supernaturally open up conversations about Jesus and our vision for an untraditional expression of church. One warm fall evening, I was out on my bicycle taking a break from the busy activities in our home, and God opened up a conversation with a man named John. He, like me, had become discouraged with church and was not attending anywhere. He and his family joined our little band, and he became one of our first elders. Another, an accountant named Vic, had his office in the same complex as Don Thomas. Don and I were meeting in his office regularly for prayer, and I got to know Vic. He had grown up Catholic and was hungry to cultivate a personal relationship with Jesus. He and his family became part of our group. Vic became our invaluable financial guru. And Don Thomas led his secretary, Audrey Hermle, to faith in Jesus, and she joined our group. Steve, the man who ran the print shop where I took my business, had gotten burned out on traditional church. He played the 12-string guitar, and offered to help us with worship music. He even owned a stand-up bass which he happily shared with me to play. Paul, a research scientist and grad student at UC Davis, read a newspaper article about the launch of Woodland Bible Church and contacted us. He believed in what we were doing and became another of our first elders. And on it went. While we were finding ways to love needy people, God was finding people to form the core of Woodland Bible Church. It was truly remarkable.

He was even working in the heart of the curmudgeonly editor of the Woodland Daily Democrat newspaper. I mentioned the fortuitous location of our home on the busy corner. One day I was sitting at my desk, watching the neighborhood parade go by our house. An idea stirred within me: "*What if I were to offer to write a short weekly column for the newspaper? Could that give some credibility and visibility to our fledgling ministry? It would certainly force me to get to know my new town. I would call it 'My Woodland Window.'*" So I wrote out four short essays, each with a similar format. I observed something about our town and its environs and then drew a Biblical application. I gathered them together and found my way to the newspaper office on Court Street, where I asked to speak with the editor. The receptionist ushered me down the hall to the office of Mr. Ken Leake.

It was a classic scene: piles of papers stacked all over his desk and all around his small office. He saw me appear in the doorway, and he pulled down his glasses to the end of his nose while he peered over the top of them at me with a disdainful expression. "Yeah, what do you need?"

"Hello, Mr. Leake, I'm Ron Kingham. I'm the pastor-teacher of a new church which is happening in Woodland. I'd like to offer to write a weekly column for your paper."

His brow furrowed. "Let me see what you've got," he said brusquely. So I handed him my samples. He glanced at them quickly and looked back at me. With a sense of dismissal, he said, "I can't pay you anything."

I replied, "That's fine. I just ask that you print the name of my church along with my name." He nodded and I left, not really sure what would become of my efforts. When I got home, Cathy prayed with me, and we left it with the Lord.

Days went by. Finally on Saturday, we opened the paper, and there was my first column—right next to his main editorial, in the upper left quadrant of the page where eyes first land! And it became a feature of the Saturday paper for the next two years! Not long after the publication of that first column, I was shopping in town, and the store clerk saw my name on my check. She looked up at me and asked, "Are you the one who writes 'My Woodland Window'?"

I nodded.

She scrunched up her nose and asked, "How did you ever get that space on Mr. Leake's sacred editorial page?" She went on to explain that she had worked for Ken Leake for several years, and he never allowed anyone to compete with his personal editorial space.

I just looked at the woman and said, "I have no idea. God did it." And He wonderfully used that weekly column to draw a number of people into our new church.

About the same time we announced our first public services, Don Thomas came to me with the news that the bank account was about empty, and he didn't have enough to pay my salary. So Cathy and I committed our need to the Lord, knowing He would provide. I still marvel at how well Cathy took these kinds of developments in stride. She had such sweet confidence in God's promise to provide our needs! Don Thomas had told his landlord Vic that I needed work, so he offered to hire me to build some shelves in his office. It only took a couple days, but while I was there, Vic told me about one of his clients, Bernie Gorman, a local farmer who needed someone to do a building project at his place.

I drove out to his farm, and he put me to work on a substantial framing project converting an old barn into a habitable office. About two days into the project, Bernie called me to come down from the roof and talk with him. He said, "Ron, I can see you know what you're doing and are going to do a good job. How long do you think it will take you?"

I replied, "I'm guessing three weeks."

He responded, "Do you mind if I pay you everything in advance?" Now I had been doing construction projects for quite a few years at this point, and I had *never* been paid in advance. But our gracious heavenly Father knew we needed the money right then, so he touched a spinach farmer in Yolo, California, to write us the check.

From the outset, I wanted both my personal life and the establishment of Woodland Bible Church to be faith ventures. Then all the glory can be given to God, and the work which is accomplished can truly be labeled a divine work. Faith is tainted with human effort when we have to ask people to give money. During seminary God bountifully provided for our needs without us ever once asking anyone (except God, of course) for money. And the same was true in the founding of WBC. Unfortunately, one of the distasteful traditions which has arisen in the Western church culture, in my opinion, is the passing of the collection plate, frequently accompanied by an extortive plea from the church leader. I had been inspired by the example of the famous nineteenth-century preacher and orphanage director George Müller. He believed God would always supply his needs without ever asking anyone. So in his church he did not pass an offering plate or basket. He simply placed a slotted box on the wall and trusted people to give as God prompted them.

Thus, as Don Thomas and I were shaping the early traditions of our non-traditional church, we agreed to a box on the table (in early days) or on the wall (once we had our own building). We printed a note in very small print in the weekly bulletin/handout which read, "If you wish to contribute to the work of Woodland Bible Church, a box is available on the back table." From the day of our first public meeting at the Women's Clubhouse in November 1978 until I finished my tenure there in the summer of 2002, our offerings were taken this way. Every time I received a salary check, I was able to joyfully say, "Thank You, Lord. You have touched Your people to supply our needs. All the glory goes to You!" Countless times I was able to utter those famous words first transmitted over the telegraph wires in 1844: "What hath God wrought!"

When I finished that project for spinach farmer Bernie Gorman, there was enough in the WBC bank account for my salary, and it never dried up again. At times when I would need extra cash, God would make work available. For example, Dr. Matthews, our dentist, offered to trade his dental work for my carpentry work. It was an exciting faith venture to watch how God consistently provided for our needs, but we seldom had excess, especially during those early years in Woodland. We were true minimalists!

Our first service at the Women's Clubhouse was amazing. A young woman named Rosemary had painted an A-frame sign with our name on it. It was parked on the sidewalk outside. There were about twenty-five adults there plus a bunch of children. Two elderly ladies, Lucy and Alice, showed up carrying their Bibles and hymnbooks, thinking a new church wouldn't have hymnals (they were right). We were high tech. We used an overhead projector with the words to songs handwritten on transparencies! Don set up chairs. Steve played guitar and I played along on the borrowed bass. Paul's wife played piano. Don led a sharing and prayer time, and I preached a sermon. Mary and Cathy took the children into the kitchen and had a Bible lesson with them. It was a beginning. And God had assembled all of us quite supernaturally.

Within six months we had outgrown the facilities at the Women's Clubhouse. Don negotiated a deal with the local Seventh Day Adventist (SDA) Church to rent their entire facility on Sundays. It provided us significant benefits. There were rooms for various classes, there was a well-furnished nursery for babies, it had a tank for doing baptisms, and it had carpet to mitigate noise. We met there for the next seven years until God swung the door open for us to buy our own facility, the former Starworld Skate Center, right in the center of town.

10

Woodland—An Introvert Raising Five Kids on a Small Income

I grew up in a "typical American family": two parents and two kids. And since my sister was five and a half years younger than I and we lived in a rural community, I knew absolutely nothing of the dynamics of a large family with all the siblings very close in age. As we began our life in Woodland, I was now the dad of a bustling, jostling, busy household where the total span between five kids was six and a half years. It was different for Cathy. She was the first of six siblings, and although they were spaced out over eighteen years, her household of origin was always a busy place. Dorchester, Massachusetts, where she grew up, was densely populated. I think she told me there were seventy kids on her little cul-de-sac when she was a kid. So with our large, busy family, she was in her element. But I was not. She was also much more balanced in her personality type. She was blessed with a pleasant mix of introversion and extroversion. I not so much. I'm pretty solidly introverted. I mostly "did relationships" because they were the necessary component of loving my neighbor in the name of Jesus, not because I drew strength and joy and energy from the social interaction. Quite the opposite, actually. To this day, social activity drains me. So you can see that I was the square peg in the round hole of this amazing family God gave me. Part of the story of God's grace at work in my life is the way He had to chisel away my weariness with craziness and fun. How many times did I hear Cathy say, "Lighten up, Ron. They're just having fun."? I look back with a measure of shame for my overly serious demeanor at times.

But this was the family God gave me. He assigned me the task of being their dad. Each of my kids was an awesome exhibit of the Creator's handiwork. So I sought His help often and listened to Cathy's guidance at every turn of the road. They deserved a dad who was very emotionally present and actively affirmative, expressing to them how extraordinary and unique they were. But it never came naturally for me. Cathy was constantly helping me see signals of needed connection with various kids.

With four boys in the home, rude noises were worshipped and idolized—you know, the kind which emanate from the secret places of the body, sometimes known as farts and burps. I tried my best to marshal disapproval, but it drove Cathy crazy. So she created a little song as punishment for the inappropriate expression of a rude noise, especially at the dinner table. When one of them would "break wind" or blast a loud burp, she would look at them with those I'm-the-mom-and-I'm-not-happy-with-you eyes, and announce, "That's rude, crude, vulgar, uncouth and utterly disgusting. Sing the song." And then the perpetrator would sing/say:

> With my voice, with my bod
> I will try to honor God
> I will not make noises that are rude
> I want to be an awesome dude

All the while, the others (*usually* not Bethany) would be quietly giggling. This was particularly egregious if it happened while we were having family devotions. I hadn't dealt with this sort of thing growing up, so it always made me wonder if our family was OK. Over time, I came to appreciate the wonder of it all. They were such happy, bright kids, and they loved laughing together.

God often took care of our needs in the most fascinating ways. One such instance happened about a year after we came to Woodland. It was my custom to wear a coat and tie on Sundays, and my suit was worn. Cathy lovingly reminded me I needed a new suit, but there was no money for that. One day we saw a newspaper ad for the grand opening of a brand new lumber yard called 84 Lumber. Cathy and I were always on the lookout for cheap/free activities to have a little fun with the kids away from home. To get the public to come and look at the new business, they were offering 10¢ sodas and hot dogs. It looked like a great chance to take the kids out to dinner for a couple bucks—and see the new lumber yard to boot. So we piled into our VW bus (which we had bought shortly after the twins were born) and drove to get our cheap eats. It was a little weird walking around with our five little kids checking out a lumber yard, but they were enjoying the outing. Then Nathan said, "Dad, they're having a contest. You ought to enter it."

I really don't enjoy contests (I'm the introvert, remember), but to humor my son I checked it out. It was a three-event competition: How fast can you saw through a 6"x6" beam with a handsaw? How fast can you drive a sixteen penny nail into a beam? And how close can you cast a fishing plug to a target on the ground? Three things which were definitely in my wheelhouse! So I entered. The kids cheered for

Dad, and to their delight, I won! The prize was $100, just what I needed for a new suit.

I'm confident that one of the reasons God provided for our needs so wonderfully was because we deliberately sought to "seek *first* His kingdom and His righteousness" (Matthew 6:33, lit. Greek). For Cathy, this meant being extremely frugal. She was a passionate expert in squeezing our dollars until they yielded double value—utilizing thrift stores, coupons, garage sales, etc. Another way was our relentless commitment to follow the principle of Proverbs 3:9-10: "Honor the Lord from your wealth, and from the *first* of all your increase, so your barns will be filled with plenty..." (lit. Hebrew). In the midst of the costly demands of raising five kids, we never wavered from our happy vow to give God significantly more than the Old Testament tithe.

I say we never wavered, but there was one moment when I almost faltered. The kids were all grammar school age, and I was working on a project on the workbench in our garage. My kids were playing outside, and the neighbor boy from across the street, Darrell, came over and joined my boys. He was all excited. He had just returned from a trip to Disneyland. He went on and on about the things they did. I listened as he talked, and I perceived the longing looks on the faces of my boys. I also silently added up the amount of money his family had spent. It was at least two thousand dollars. I felt words start to form in my mouth. I was about to say, "We could take our family there too, if we didn't give so much to God." But, thankfully, something put a plug in my throat just as those words started to come out.

In a flash—right there at my workbench in the garage—I was painfully aware I had resentment in my heart. Without saying a word, I quietly left and sequestered myself in my study for a while and had a serious talk with God. I confessed that it was hard to raise a big family on such a small income. I faced the truth that I had drifted into being a resentful giver instead of the cheerful giver He wanted me to be (2 Corinthians 9:7). Then I rehearsed the clear call God had placed on me, and asked for His help to trust Him with our finances. I cried out for His help to figure out ways to have family fun without the expense of Disneyland! As I look back, I am exceedingly grateful for that moment at the workbench. It was a test of my resolve to continue to live by faith with a cheerful heart.

God provided for our family in little ways and big ways. People would bring us fresh produce from the area farms, and even a whole butchered lamb on two occasions. One Christmas when I didn't have money to buy a Christmas tree, I found one discarded in the street and recycled it. When our VW bus reached the end of its useful life, we began to pray for God's provision for a new vehicle. God answered by touching a dear friend to send us a check for $10,000 with which we purchased a low mileage Ford E-150 eight-passenger full-sized van. We ran the wheels off that van!

All five of our kids attended Woodland Christian School from K-8th grade. It was, in large measure, a God-send for us. Dear friends and family lovingly helped us at times with the tuition. The school was close by—the kids all walked, or rode bikes, or skateboarded their way to school. We lived for ten years with only one car, and so it was a blessing that they could get themselves to school. Academically the school was top-notch. Spiritually, the school was a bit disappointing because it often taught more about the cultural rules of good moral behavior than the joy of a vibrant faith in the living Jesus. But WCS was a great place for our kids to learn discipline and hard work. They also were able to learn music skills. Cathy and I started each of our kids at age six on the piano. This provided them the rudiments of music theory. Then at WCS they each branched out into band instruments: Nathan—trombone, Jonathan—trumpet, Bethany—bells/glockenspiel, Peter—trumpet, and Andrew—French horn. There was a year when all five were in the band at WCS. We had them doing their practicing right after they got up in the morning. The music/cacophony coming from our house was... well, cacophony. I'm amazed my neighbors never complained. Then as our kids started through the stages of puberty, they started branching out. The music which was instilled in them from those early days blossomed into phenomenal skills in singing, song writing, and various stringed and percussive instruments. When their mother passed away from cancer in 2017, they sang and played for her memorial service. One man told me afterward that their music was the best he had ever heard *anywhere*. Thank God that in those early days, music was very much a part of our home.

Of course Cathy, the woman who was created to be a mom, was always setting the pace for a fun and educational home environment. She was inventing games, reading books, taking the kids on outings to the local parks, having them memorize scriptures, and making projects for friends and family, etc. Remember, we had no TV. While other kids were zoned out staring at the Tube, Cathy was busily engaging our kids' minds with fun and useful activities. I would periodically take the kids fishing. For a couple years (before the evil time keepers messed with the date for the spring-forward time change), I would rouse them from sleep before dawn in the spring and throw them in the VW bus. We would drive out to Knights Landing to a place on the Sacramento River where we could fish for striped bass for a couple hours *before* school. I have sweet memories of seeing them hook a striper and play it in to shore. And I tried to keep up with their development athletically. I installed a slam-dunk basketball hoop in the driveway at one point, and I built a "quarter-pipe" ramp for skateboarding and roller skates.

We wanted our kids to learn the joy and necessity of work. So early on, Cathy started them on chores around the house. Every night they had assigned tasks for cleaning up after dinner. And as they grew big enough we found them jobs to earn money, like yard work and paper routes. On occasion I would take the boys with me on a for-money work project like building a fence or re-roofing a house so they could "earn and learn." They often accompanied me to cut and load firewood. Bethany earned money for a while picking up litter outside an office complex in town. From this vantage point in my old age, I can certainly see the results of these early exposures to work. Praise God, our adult kids are all hard-working, responsible citizens, providing for their families and mostly working in areas of their strengths and passions. Though at times they resisted the training, they are living testimonies to the truth of Hebrews 12:11 which says: "No discipline seems pleasant at the time, but painful. Later on, however, it produces a harvest of righteousness and peace for those who have been trained by it" (NIV).

As the large-family dynamic played out, Cathy and I both realized that our days were full of interactions with the group, but not necessarily full of interactions with the individual kids. So we sought the Lord for wisdom, and He gave Cathy an idea: How about Dad takes each kid out for a special date/outing on their "half birthday"—their birthday plus six months. Thus began a tradition which lasted several years to plan and carry out special events for each one on their half birthday. I remember Bethany at about age seven all dressed up for a date with Daddy. We went out for dinner, visited a small aquarium, and watched a movie together. I remember taking my twins up into the control tower of Sacramento International Airport and having them put on head sets and actually talk to the planes which were taking off and landing. (You can't do that anymore!) I was constantly searching for cheap/free outings. One time I took someone (I can't remember which kid) to the tomato testing station. Huge double semi loads of freshly picked tomatoes would come to be tested before heading for the ketchup factory. We laughed for years afterwards when we learned the true meaning of the ingredient on the ketchup label that says "natural flavors." We learned that that was an acceptable amount of M. O. T. (material other than tomatoes, i.e. sticks, dirt, rodents, and snakes). Had it not been for Cathy's wisdom, I may have missed these opportunities completely. What a gift was my sweet Cathy!

Cathy also cautiously dodged the cultural pressure to have huge expensive birthday parties for the kids. She conceived a plan to do big parties only when the kids turned five, ten, and thirteen. For five and ten we invited all their friends and employed all the usual extravagances of children's birthday parties. At thirteen we saved up our money for a special night out with Mom and Dad. We got dressed up and took them out for a fancy dinner theater or restaurant. All other birthdays were very Spartan: simply a cake and a couple gifts.

Since the church at that time only had rented space on Sundays, I worked out of our home. It became apparent very early that we needed more room for the kids to spread out and

154

me to have a private office/study. So in June of 1980, we designed and built a second story above the garage. This added six hundred square feet for an office, a game room, and most importantly a third bathroom. The upstairs became a huge part of the family dynamic which comprised the Kingham household for the next two decades. What a blessing it was! We were enabled by God to complete the whole project with a $6,000 second mortgage which a brother from church loaned us. In a few years, we were able to refinance the whole house, reduce our mortgage payment, and pay off the second. It was financial transactions like this that had the fingerprints of God's providence written all over them!

As the kids grew, our home became an even busier, noisier, happier place. Our location on the corner made us a natural place for neighbors, friends, and church people to gather. Cathy worked hard to preserve family dinner. We believed it was vital to gather everyone around the table both morning and evening. Since we had mostly boys, there was constant good-natured (mostly!) wrangling, competing, challenging, shoulder-pounding, and talking in strange invented languages. It was the kind of thing I had never experienced in my family of origin, so it often left me wondering if it was good or bad. When you add in the point that an introvert derives energy from peace and solitude, you can see my dilemma. It is only in retrospect that I have fully come to appreciate now how good it was. My adult children are well-balanced people with the resilience to handle the bumps of life around them.

Sports were a constant source of conflict for me. Since I knew how important my year of football in high school had been in the development of my self-awareness as a man, I was supportive of my kids playing sports. But many contemporary families were allowing sports to absolutely dominate their homes, and I didn't want that. So Cathy and I cautiously navigated the treacherous waters of sports involvement. Nathan became quite skilled in soccer, actually receiving a scholarship for his first year of college. Jonathan dabbled in soccer, basketball, and football. Bethany was an outstanding volleyball player, and the twins excelled in skateboarding and roller hockey. I didn't get to all of their games as I would have liked because of ministry conflicts, but I did manage to get to quite a few of them.

One memory stands out. Since Jonathan knew how to kick a soccer ball, he made the football team as the place-kicker. His coach didn't believe in kicking field goals very often, so Jon saw limited action. But on a cold Friday night in November in the pouring rain, his team drove the ball into field goal range. It was fourth down. The driving rain made it hard to see at times as Cathy and I watched from the bleachers. The coach sent in the kicker! You could see by the way Jon ran onto the field that he had visions of three points dancing in his head. He took his place behind the holder. The center snapped the wet ball, but it was way off target. Jon ran to his right and grabbed the loose ball. He got it safely in his clutches, and now he had visions of *six* points dancing in his head! He started running towards the goal. Two defenders converged on him from opposite sides and hit him with the force of a Mack truck. They sent him sliding like an otter across the muddy field spraying water like a water skier. No six points. And thankfully, no broken bones. Once we were certain he was OK, we started laughing. Thirty years later I still laugh when I reconstitute the image of that water slide!

When we were approaching ten years at WBC, Cathy and I began dreaming about a serious sabbatical—a road trip around the whole United States. We received permission from the elders to take off the entire summer of 1988. We prayerfully strategized how we could possibly do such an audacious thing. We came up with a plan to live even more frugally for the year prior and save all that money for our trip. I look back with great delight as I remember all the cost-cutting maneuvers we employed. We were able to save around $12,000. With that money we got the VW engine rebuilt, fitted it with a trailer hitch and bought a used pop-up tent trailer. It was designed to sleep six (we were seven). Poor Bethany drew the middle spot between stinky teenage brothers. Cathy outfitted the trailer so we could live on the road. We were quite a sight: Brown and white VW bus with the front spare tire cover reading "Thy Kinghams come" pulling a tent trailer with a couple young heads bobbing above the sun roof. We were gone the whole summer. We drove the southern route all the way to Orlando, Florida, where we took in Disneyworld. Then up the east coast to Boston to spend time with Cathy's relatives there. Then across to Niagara Falls and the northern tier of states into Montana. From there we found our way back home.

I could fill a book with stories just about our sabbatical adventure. But let me share just one story which illustrates the way God provided for us on that entire trip. We had just completed camping for a couple days in Glacier National Park in Montana. We were packed and rolling down Highway 93 on the northwest shore of Flathead Lake. As we started up a grade, I pushed the clutch to downshift. There was a cracking sound, and I realized the clutch cable had snapped. I pulled to the side of the road and got out to assess our situation: barren landscape all around us with the lake visible below us, and very infrequent vehicles on the road. This was before cell phones. I shot up a quick "arrow" prayer: "Lord, help us figure out what to do."

The kids piled out. I was looking under the bus and had just spotted the broken cable when a car pulled up behind us. A man and woman got out and came over to ask us if we needed help. We explained our predicament. The man (I am so sorry I don't remember his name!) said, "You can come to our spread and stay with us for as long as it takes to order the part and get it repaired for you."

I was flabbergasted. "OK," I said, "Thank you so much. But how do we get this rig to your place?"

"No problem. I'll drive it for you. I'm a Montana farmer and rancher. I drive a lot of big equipment." So he proceeded to drive our clutchless VW bus towing the trailer back to his spread. I sat next to him mesmerized as I witnessed him skillfully shift without a clutch.

We were there for three days, camping on their property. It took that long to get a cable delivered to the parts store in Kalispell. During those three days, they brought us homemade jams and jellies, took us with them to a family steak barbecue, and generally gave us everything we needed. They were proud to have us there! Our kids returned the favor by doing musical performances. On the third day, when the cable arrived, a mechanic whom our host knew from town, came out and installed the new part. As the whole episode was playing out, at times it felt surreal. Only God could touch people to be so generous and kind. When we got home, we ordered a California fruit and nut tray and had it shipped to the folks in Kalispell. But we never got confirmation that they received it. For a long time afterwards, we wondered if we had been the recipients of an angelic visitation.

I believe an angel of protection did indeed visit me in Woodland once. Bethany was about three. This was before the seat belt laws. She was sitting on the front passenger seat across from me in the VW bus, her cute blond pig tails dancing in the sunlight. She had accompanied me on an errand in town. We were driving south on West Street. I started to make the left turn onto El Dorado when I heard her door unlatch. I was going about twenty-five miles per hour, and at that speed the centrifugal force started pulling the door wide open. As I looked, horrified, the swinging door was pulling her *out of the car!* With my feet on the clutch and the brake, my right arm shot across to her, grabbed her by the arm and pulled her in just before she contacted the pavement. In God's grace there were no other cars in the intersection. I stopped and moved over to close and lock her door—and to let my heart slow down after the adrenaline rush. I hugged her and gently reminded her not to touch the door handle. We drove on home, and I told Cathy what had happened. Then I went back out into the VW bus and re-enacted the incident. No matter what I did, I could not keep my feet on the pedals and get anywhere near where she had been going out the swinging door. My arm needed another three feet. To this day, I remain convinced God sent an angel to momentarily lengthen my arm to save precious Bethany's life.

Cathy persisted in being a stay-at-home mom, focusing her energy on our family and on her many ministries at our growing church. But when the twins reached Junior High age, she felt it was time to augment our income by going back to nursing. She got herself re-certified and took a position as an RN at Woodland Memorial Hospital. Rather quickly she gravitated to her area of personal interest and passion, mental health. So from about 1987 until she was diagnosed with cancer in 2009, she worked as a psychiatric nurse. She was extremely good at what she did. She loved her patients with the love of Jesus. Somehow (once again, it had to be God's providential care), she was one of the only employees at WMH who was given the privilege of working just two days a week and yet receiving full benefits—for the whole family! And nurses are paid quite well! So for those twenty-two years, Cathy worked the most amazing schedule: four-days-on, ten-days-off. This became a huge blessing after we moved to Oroville. With her benefits, we had health insurance. Up until she went back to nursing, we had been paying for our health care needs out of pocket. So her employment was a blessing to her patients and a blessing to our family. And she was home for ten days at a time!

The reason I was without any healthcare coverage was that I had specifically asked the elders of WBC to not pay for any insurance or any retirement plan. I wanted them to plow that money into the ministries of our church instead of my personal needs. I believed God would take care of us. And He did! From 1978 to 1987, He faithfully enabled us to pay for the things that came up. And with five active kids, believe me, things came up! Once Cathy went to work at the hospital, we had excellent coverage. And then when she had to quit because of her cancer, it was the exact time for us to go on Medicare. God took care of us all the way along. I will talk about the absence of any retirement plan in a later chapter, as it is yet another of the many incredible stories of His gracious provision in my life.

One of my most poignant and painful family memories was the Yosemite Fire in August of 1990. It was our custom to spend the two weeks just before school began in the fall at our cabin in Yosemite. That year, we were really pumped to have a wonderful time in the mountains. Nathan had just graduated from high school and this could be one of our last times together for family vacation. We packed up our van, loaded the tent trailer, and even packed up a second vehicle which Tom and Donna Horgan had given us, an old 1964 Buick battleship affectionately known as "The Boat." We caravanned to Yosemite. As we pulled up to the turnoff for Foresta, just ten minutes from the cabin, we were stopped by a park ranger. He said, "There's a fire coming up out of the Merced River canyon, and you can't go in there."

So we turned around and went up the hill to a turnout which looked out over Foresta. We saw the fire come bursting over the crest of the plateau igniting one-hundred-fifty foot pine trees like they were matches. To say we were shocked would be an understatement. It was the most horrific scene I have ever witnessed. That fire wound up destroying many thousands of acres of gorgeous Sierra wilderness, and it consumed our little cabin. It took us two days to finally be ushered out of the park while we left most of our gear behind. After the fire was stopped, we were able to reclaim our things, but the cabin was history. As the reality of that dreadful experience came home to roost, it became symbolic of the change which must happen as life plays out. The kids missed the cabin, but I felt the loss most deeply because it had been part of my life for thirty-four years. I hadn't dealt with much loss in my life, and this was a big wound. We tried to ease the pain a few years later by commissioning an artist to paint a huge (3'x7') watercolor. That painting has become a family treasure. Jonathan has the original, and all the siblings and I have prints. Mine is hanging on the wall above me as I compose these words. I can't go the cabin anymore, but I can savor the memories as I gaze in sweet reverie.

When each of the kids reached 9th grade, they switched over to the public school system at Woodland High School (WHS). Cathy, of course, was extremely vigilant, so she became active in the WHS PTA for the years our kids were there. She worked diligently to hold the thumb in the dike of moral decline at the school. Just as an example of the changes in public high school in the twenty-six years between my graduation and Nathan's graduation, consider this contrast: I was appointed student body president because the elected president got his girlfriend pregnant in 1963. Nathan told me that the student body president of WHS in 1989 boasted around campus on Mondays about whom she slept with over the weekend. I really think Cathy's efforts were meaningful, but it was a constant battle.

As each kid made the transition to the public high school, he/she was exposed to much more of the atheistic philosophies and values of this world. Cathy and I continued to teach and model the world view which is rooted in the belief that God created everything and lovingly redeemed His erring creatures with the death of Jesus on the cross. But all of my five kids, to varying degrees, were impacted by this clash of world views. Cathy and I fought to find time to pray together for them, realizing that once they reached this time of adolescence and pre-adulthood, our parental role needed to shift away from being teachers to being pray-ers. I have honest regrets, however, that in our busy lives, we didn't fight hard enough to prioritize more time for intercession on behalf of our children. One of the wonderful blessings of the last few years (as I write this in my early 70s) is the confidence my adult children and grandchildren can have knowing that I have deepened my commitment to pray daily for them. Prayer has become a huge part of my life as a senior! Thank God for His merciful patience and love as I have grown.

God bestowed a huge honor upon me when He sent Nathan, Jonathan, Bethany, Peter, and Andrew into our home to be our children. The challenge and responsibility of being their parents was huge! It was fun, hard, exhausting (especially for a morning person who folds up his tent so early in the evening), thrilling, perplexing, and scary—all at the same time. How many times did Cathy and I face situations which brought us before the Throne of Grace seeking wisdom for what to do as their parents? God only knows. But I am grateful He walked with us through the whole journey. And despite our countless mistakes, He enabled us to launch them all into healthy, productive adulthood. I am so proud of my children! Psalm 127:3-6 says: "Children are a heritage from the LORD, offspring a reward from him. Like arrows in the hands of a warrior are children born in one's youth. Blessed is the man whose quiver is full of them" (NIV). When I was studying in seminary, I learned that the warriors of ancient times often carried five arrows in their quiver. I truly am a blessed man with a full quiver!

11

Woodland Bible Church—the Vision Realized

Our fledgling church began meeting at the Seventh Day Adventist facility in the spring of 1979. By that time the Lord had led about fifty committed people into the WBC family. We never had a formal membership roll because the elders did not believe membership is mentioned in the Bible. We simply collected contact information so we could be a family and keep in touch. Those early meetings were pretty unkempt and unpolished—and in fact they never did get polished throughout my twenty-four years there! That was part of the genius of the early days of WBC. People felt free to enter into the dynamic of body life. They didn't put on pretenses or Sunday demeanor. Our services typically followed the format of about an hour of praise, worship and body life sharing (led by an elder or leader in development), followed by a fifteen-minute coffee break, and then finished with about forty-five minutes of teaching from the scriptures (usually by me). The children were present with us for the first hour and then would be ushered off to their own teaching time.

The SDA facility was small enough that we didn't need a microphone for sharing time. But when we moved into our larger permanent home on California Street, we had a volunteer runner passing the mic. Sharing time was always such a blessing to me. It was like opening a window into the spiritual lives of our people. It gave us a sweet opportunity to come alongside each other in victories, defeats, pain, and growth. It caused the flock to learn transparency, love, and forgiveness instead of criticism and condemnation. It meant the people present were participants and not just observers. This was brought home quite dramatically to me one week, not long after we occupied the SDA building. An older gentleman visited us for the first time and sat silently in the back corner. I greeted him during the coffee break time and got his phone number. I paid him a visit later that week in his home. After our cordial greetings, he got to the point. He said, "Ron, I really like what you are doing there, but I won't be back."

"OK. May I ask why?" I queried.

"Because I can see that I can't just attend and be a watcher. I'm not ready to open up like that."

I replied, "We are sorry you won't be with us, but I'm glad you perceived the simplicity and power of the early church body life." As I rode my bicycle home that morning, I remember thanking God He was raising up the church I had envisioned.

As the weeks and months went by, the flock continued to grow—both spiritually and in numbers. Many of our new people were newcomers to Woodland, others were brand new believers whom our people led to Christ. We added small group Bible studies, and I started building into the young men whom God brought into our fellowship. I would meet them one-on-one wherever we could connect. For about ten years I led a year-long leadership development class. My goal was to equip young men to become godly leaders in their homes and in Jesus' church, especially as elders at WBC. Cathy would take their wives and work with them separately. This leadership development was one of the most important things I did during my years at WBC.

I was blessed just a few months ago when I had the privilege of seeing one of those men, Paul Day, who was in my leadership development class many years ago. Paul sought me out at a funeral we were both attending, and he told me he was taking young men through a similar program right now. I was thrilled, but I reminded him it wasn't my idea! I was only seeking to follow the Apostle Paul's example and instructions in 2 Timothy 2:2: "The things which you have heard from me in the presence of many witnesses, entrust these to faithful men who will be able to teach others also" (NASB). There are at least a score of men of God still serving in His kingdom who were participants in those early WBC leadership development classes.

One year I had an exceptionally responsive and hungry group of six men. They met together in the upper room at my home on the corner from September to May. I was particularly excited about launching them all into various avenues of ministry in our growing church. On the last evening, they each shared separately how helpful the class had been. And then they *each* revealed, somewhat sheepishly, how their jobs were forcing them to move away from Woodland! I was shocked! I remember complaining quite bitterly to God, "Why did I just pour my life into those guys for this whole year? How do I find leaders for WBC?"

And then, in one of those wonderful moments of epiphany, God spoke quite clearly to me and said, "Ron, this isn't about you or Woodland Bible Church. This is about *My* kingdom. You just unleashed six men into My kingdom. I'm building WBC, remember, not you. Remain faithful."

Our God exists outside of time. That was about 1982. After thirty years, I received a phone call. "Hey Ron, this is Brad Mumm. Do you remember me from WBC days?"

"Yeah," I said, somewhat incredulous, "Where are you?" (Brad had been part of that group of six who all left Woodland).

"Well, I'm in Colorado, but I'm going to be in Sacramento in a couple days, and I'd like to stop by and see you and Cathy."

We set up a lunch date, and soon we grayheads were sharing a reunion on the deck of our place in Oroville. I was bawling as Brad thanked me for my input in that class years earlier. He said, "I wanted to thank you in person. God used you powerfully in my life. What you planted in me took root. I let the world's values seduce me for a number of years, but God called me back. Now I'm in full-time Christian ministry with Athletes in Action." I'm so glad God enlarged my narrow selfish thinking back in 1982! And thirty years later He sent Brad to confirm it!

Baptisms were special times at WBC. During our SDA tenure, we did the baptizing on site in their built-in tank. Once we acquired the Starworld Skating Rink, we switched to off-site baptisms in swimming pools and the frigid American River in Sacramento. An early WBC baptism stands out. I mentioned previously, that our founding elder, Don Thomas, led his personal secretary, Audrey Hermle, to Christ. Audrey kept her faith quiet for a while, but finally felt the Spirit compel her to make it public through baptism. She hadn't quite figured out how to share her faith with her husband, Chuck. So she told him about the upcoming baptism and invited him to come hear her testimony. I can still see him as he tried to slip in unnoticed and found a seat in the very back of the room. But as Audrey gave her sweet testimony of new-found love for Jesus, I watched (from the water in the tank) as Chuck was visibly shaken. The Spirit of God reached into Chuck's heart as he watched his precious wife go under the water. As I recall, he had planned to slip out as soon as the baptism was over, but he didn't. When the service was over, I approached Chuck, and he was ready to receive Jesus right on the spot. It was a supernatural moment.

It was all about the people God sent to us. Jesus was truly building His church. They came from many walks of life, and they latched onto the governing principles we espoused from the beginning. They were (1) *evangelizers*, sharing their faith in their friendship networks (what is called in modern church parlance their *oikos*) and their families. One woman, Nancy Freschauf, who was a dental hygienist, led several of her patients to Christ. They were (2) *servers*, using their widely varied spiritual gifts to carry on all kinds of ministries to the church family and the community. They ministered to our children and youth. They shared their musical talents with the body. For several years they operated a food and clothes ministry to the homeless and needy. They were (3) *hungry learners*, gobbling up the various Bible study ministries we offered. They were (4) *creative presenters*, dreaming up wonderful imaginative presentations. One woman, Michelle Booth, wrote original Biblical dramas that the church body acted out. For many years, we held "The WBC Family Christmas Program." It was one of the most amazing displays of family bonding and creative showmanship ever to hit the stage or screen. It was totally amateurish and hokey and yet at the same time deliciously endearing. You had to be there to appreciate it. But it was possible because the people of WBC were all in. They were the body, and they all had a part.

One man, Brad Montgomery, stands out in my mind because he represented all four of the above categories. Brad was running from God as fast as a man can run. But Bonnie, his wife, and their two kids, Chelsea and Seth (both suffering from cystic fibrosis), prayed fervently for him to find Jesus. So did our church body. One Sunday he surprised everyone by accepting Chelsea's invitation to join the family at our worship service. God reached down and saved Brad that day, and his life was transformed. He had been an atheistic evolutionist. He became a hungry student of the scriptures and an ardent advocate for young earth creationism. Then he came to me one day and offered to start teaching a class on creationism! What a glorious transformation. In many ways, Brad was a symbol of the miracles God was doing through the agency of Woodland Bible Church.

The elders recognized I needed help, so starting with a part-time administrative assistant, they enlarged our staff by hiring people who became my dear partners in the work. First it was a secretary (Sharon Freeman, later Lynda Newman), then a nursery worker to free up moms to attend services, then a youth pastor (Ron Poarch, later Casey Frye), then an associate teacher and counselor (Randy Williams). But even though we had these paid staff people, WBC was always about the people of the body.

Since construction was part of the fabric of my being, God showed me how valuable it was in demonstrating the meaning of body life among the people of WBC. Most everybody has a house, and houses need fixing and remodeling. So people feel loved when their toilet or fence or roof or faucet or door gets fixed by a brother in the body. One day I received a call from one of the families in the church. Their daughter was suffering from frightening nightmares, and they wanted to know if I could help. I said I'd be right over. I got on my bicycle, rode across town, and walked up to their house. I knocked on the front door, and I saw the dad motioning to me from a window to go around to the side door. So I did. I shared and prayed with the family for some time. Then I got up to leave. As I started for the front door, they reminded me I had to go out the side door. I asked, "What's wrong with your door?"

They answered, "It's been stuck for a long time."

So I took a quick look at the door and asked, "Do you mind if I come back and fix it for you?"

"Can you?" they asked with a measure of unbelief.

I said, "Yes, my dad taught me the old 'hinge trick.' Let me go change my clothes and get my tools, and I'll be back."

So I returned an hour later and quickly repaired their front door. I can still see the precious homeschool family all clumped together in rapt awe as their long-broken door began to swing sweetly and close "ker-thump." They later reported the nightmares had stopped, but they were equally blessed their door still worked! My construction experience became even more significant when we began morphing the skating rink into a worship and body life center.

As WBC matured, so also did my personal interests and passions such as fishing, building, keeping bees, photography, drama, and wildflowers. All of them found their way into the texture of my teaching ministry. My love of fishing, building, and bees provided great sermon illustrations. I used my camera to regularly prepare slides to illustrate my teaching (this was before PowerPoint and videos). I had learned the incredible value of teaching with visuals in one of my classes at seminary. And I used my close-up lens to photograph scores of wildflowers each spring. Many times we illustrated a Psalm or a song with my slides of wildflowers. I mentioned previously about the impact of those dramatic sermons where I costumed-up and portrayed a Biblical character. This was all about wanting to make my teaching clear and compelling. As I look back (having heard from scores of WBC "alums"), I can see that God graciously used these techniques to make it happen.

Early in my days in Woodland, a brand new passion burgeoned in my heart for the Shroud of Turin. I was reading the June 1980 issue of *National Geographic*, and I was captivated by the full color spread on the Shroud—which until that moment I had never even heard of. A team of scientific researchers were reporting on their recent five-day intense study of the ancient piece of cloth purported to be the burial cloth of Jesus. I was fascinated to learn that the picture of the man on the Shroud was *actually* a photographic negative—which I knew was something quite remarkable if an artist had painted it before photography was invented, as skeptics alleged. But then I read that the researchers had scanned the image on the cloth with the V-8 Analyzer, the *same* V-8 Analyzer which I was familiar with from my time at Itek ten years before! That got my attention! The V-8 Analyzer used the physics principle that the intensity of light varies proportionately with the inverse square of its distance from the source. For example, twice as far away, the light is four times dimmer. I knew the V-8 Analyzer would only produce a 3-D image of a photograph of something which was originally in 3-D. If it scanned a hand drawn painting made in 2-D, the analyzer would simply produce "noise." When the Shroud was scanned, it had produced a 3-D image! Thus began my lifelong adventure of studying the Shroud and sharing slide shows with inquisitive audiences. I became a passionate advocate of the

172

Shroud partly because of my scientific background, and partly because I had originally cinched my faith-decision in Jesus on the basis of the resurrection. And the Shroud of Turin is compelling scientific evidence for the explosive power and reality of the resurrection of Jesus!

However, none of the above passions could hold a candle to the growing passion that accumulated within me concerning the importance of the Lord's Table, the communion. Very early in my time at WBC, I became captivated with the significance and centrality of the Table. Jesus Himself told us that it is *His* divinely appointed means for us to remember Him, and as such it becomes the ultimate pathway to worship. Jesus is the "radiance of God's glory and the exact representation of His nature" (Hebrews 1:3, NASB). So I supposed that the lustrous facets of His glory must be inexhaustible. Thus it was that one day, early in my tenure at WBC, I challenged God to give me something absolutely brand new (to me) and fresh *every time* we gathered around the Table. My goal was to help the flock see the magnificent radiance of His glory, and to respond by ordering their lives accordingly. I am so grateful God put this hunger in my heart!

Our times around the Table at WBC became memorable moments of seeing glimpses of Jesus' glory. I resolved to devote special energy and time to the preparation and carrying out of our communion services. I grew in my understanding of the nature of human memory. I learned the crucial importance of synesthesia—invoking all the five senses to create accurate memories which endure. Every time we gathered around the bread and cup at WBC (for twenty-four years), and every time I have helped groups celebrate the Table ever since, God has lovingly given me a fresh look at Jesus. It has been absolutely amazing. I am more in love with Jesus and

His Table today than ever before. This passion for the Table continually gathered steam through all my years in Woodland, and finally drove a writing project which I started when I left WBC, and completed in 2013 with the publication *of Glimpses of Glory, A Leader's Guide to Remembering Jesus at the Communion Table* (Stonehaven Press, 2013). I wanted to help other church leaders unearth the buried treasure which lies largely covered up by rote and empty traditions. (Yes, the book is available at *amazon.com*.)

After several years in the SDA facility, which was only available on Sundays, we began to hear increasing talk about our need for a place of our own which we could occupy 24/7. The elders appointed a committee to begin searching for property, a long story that played out over a couple years. But I want to share a couple the key highlights which underscore God's miraculous intervention on our behalf. The Relocation Committee scoured Woodland for a place where our little rag-tag group could settle, but everywhere they looked seemed way beyond our means. People had been contributing to a designated building fund, and we had about $75,000 in hand. Sometime in 1985, they checked out the Starworld Skate Center near the corner of California and Main Streets. It had been sitting vacant for several years. The owners, a large corporate developer in Sacramento, Pannetoni Developments, had it for sale for $800,000. But skating rinks had gone out of vogue shortly after this one was built, and there were no buyers. The committee and elders agreed it was out of our league. So it was passed by. A year went by, and the committee was still searching. They revisited the skating rink. The owners were getting desperate, evidently, because they had lowered the asking price to $600,000. By now we had saved about $150,000, but that would still mean an indebtedness of $450,000, a horrible burden to place upon the backs of our little group.

The elders and the church prayed earnestly about this opportunity. The seller was ready to carry the financing (at a whopping twelve percent; remember, it was 1986) without any co-signers on the loan, a requirement we felt was crucial based on the clear teaching of Proverbs (6:1-3, 11:15, 17:18). The people met and held a prayer vigil in the parking lot of the skating rink. There was a unanimous sense from the Lord that this was a faith step He wanted us to take. So the committee wrote a formal offer, but—whether advertently or inadvertently, I'll never know—the offer was written up at $500,000. We received word that the offer was signed, and God had blessed us with our own building! This meant that our facilities expenses jumped from $300 per month (to rent the SDA building) to $3,000 per month plus utilities, etc. A more than tenfold jump! I remember praying, "Lord, this is huge. Please provide our needs and help us not lose the vibrancy of our body life."

We would be paying interest only and had a huge balloon payment due in five years. But it was our place. God was stretching my faith way beyond anything I had ever experienced before. And to my delight and amazement, God touched our people to increase what they put into the offering box, and He infused our treasury with the funds needed to make that huge jump in the budget. I am still amazed at that miracle.

Thus began the slow, exciting, scary saga of the transformation of the skating rink into a marvelous center for the multifaceted body life ministry of Woodland Bible Church. I joined the elders in attempting to cast the vision for the potential of this huge 20,000 square foot facility. But we also tried to make it clear that we would not let the building project sap the life out of our people. That's why the project proceeded slowly. We moved as money came in and people were available to do the work. Ed Thorpe, a young architect in our body volunteered to draw up plans for the conversion. I assumed the role of construction supervisor, securing materials and organizing countless workdays. The first workday was memorable. The skating rink was surrounded by a three-foot high concrete block wall which we dismantled with a jackhammer. The walls were covered with an ugly, dark blue carpet. All of it needed to go away. One of the men in the church had a VW bug which was small enough to drive through the double doors. I can still see the carpet being ripped off the walls as it was towed by the VW bug.

Once we stripped the rink bare, we began the gargantuan task of re-building it into a new facility. We cordoned off one third of the building and rented it out (for $800 per month—a major help to our budget!) to a local appliance company as their warehouse. The other two thirds became the new home of WBC. The project took us a full ten years to complete. The work was all done by our people, and we paid for it as we went along. So for a long time we conducted church activities in a bare and unfinished facility. There was a long stretch when we were in a building with unpainted sheetrock and bare openings without doors.

A story which became emblematic of our life in an unfinished facility bears telling. One Saturday, I helped a brother hang sheetrock in his house which he was remodeling. His wife took the kids away for the day. It had been in the open-studs stage for a while, so the wallboard made quite a change. When the mom returned home, she asked her little three-year-old what she thought about it. With wide eyes she exclaimed, "It looks like a church!" (I think she actually said, "It wooks wike a choich.")

You can imagine our uneasiness as we approached the five year point on our loan with Pannetoni Development Company. A huge balloon payment was due, and we didn't have the money to pay it. The building had become a wonderful asset to our ministry, but now it was quickly becoming a liability. The elders agreed that the spiritual life of our body was much more important than our investment in an earthly facility. So we contacted a local realtor and signed a contract to list it for sale. I'll never forget the feeling in the pit of my stomach when the realtor said, "This place will go quickly. I can think of three buyers who are looking for this place."

I silently acquiesced to the Lord, *"OK, Lord, you can have it, but I'm am going to be very sad to let it go."*

Days went by, and the realtor didn't show the building. In fact, no realtor ever showed it once for the entire ninety-day life of the contract! So we had a clue from the Lord He wasn't going to let us lose it. Then the elders called the church to a time of prayer and fasting. We asked them to call on God to either sell the building if we didn't need it any more or to work miraculously to rescue it from it being foreclosed by the note holder. I personally started a fast. When you don't eat, you have time to think clearly about why you are fasting. I kept talking with God about the building. I would walk around inside and remember all the wonderful things which were happening in the worship center, the nursery, the children's rooms, the food and clothes give-away closet, the kitchen, the "Spice Room"—where Cathy had a powerful ministry with women. I would recall wonderful communion services, powerful music by the worship band, Passover dinners, people I had counseled in my office…. In the midst of one of those days during my fast, I had to get up from my desk and use the restroom. (I'm sorry if this grosses you out, but I must tell the story as it actually happened.) I was standing at the urinal, and I looked up towards heaven and I cried out loud, "Lord, what do you want us to do about this building?"

Instantly I heard His voice clearly say, "Call Pannetoni. Tell them your situation."

I had never spoken to our lenders. The treasurer and the committee had always been the interface with Pannetoni. It's way outside my comfort zone to complain or beg, but I had heard a clear word from the Lord. So I walked back into my study and found the phone number and dialed them up while I cried "Help" to my Lord. My heart was pounding in my chest as I got Rod Sargeant on the line. We exchanged formalities, and then I got to my business. "Rod, you know we've been absolutely faithful in making our monthly payments on our loan. We have seen a wonderful church family spring to life in this former skating rink, and we really aren't ready to let the building go. But we are simply not in a position to make the big balloon payment which is due in a couple months." I stopped.

He thought for a moment, and then said, "We have indeed appreciated your responsible payments. Let me see what I can do. Nice talking with you."

I hung up the phone having no idea what had just happened, but I knew I had obeyed the voice of God. About two days later, my secretary said I had a call from Rod Sargeant with Pannetoni Developments. I picked up the phone. "Ron, here's all I can do. How about we re-write the note for another five years, drop your interest from twelve percent to eight percent, and we give Woodland Bible Church a gift of

$125,000 ($25,000 per year for five years) off your principal. Will that help you?"

I could hardly speak. I managed something like, "Oh, my goodness. Bless you. That will certainly make the difference! God used you to answer our prayer."

The news quickly spread around the body that the Lord had answered us in our time of prayer and fasting with a resounding exclamation point of blessing! But He wasn't finished. About three days later we received a call from A-1 Appliance Company. They were our tenants in the west third of our building. The voice said, "Hey Ron, we hear WBC's having financial difficulties. We love our warehouse. How about we raise our rent from $800 to $1,200 per month? Will that help you?"

"Wow. Bless you! That will help indeed!" When was the last time you heard of a tenant voluntarily upping their own rent? So when all the numbers were crunched, we had dropped our monthly facilities expense by a net $1,400 and secured the facility for another five years. And by the time that second note came due, we were able to refinance the whole package at an even lower rate with an amortized mortgage paying down the principle. God had miraculously saved the facility. To Him be the glory! Again!

In the summer of 1994, Cathy and I received a visit from one of my classmates at seminary, Luke Bose, from Vijayawada, Andrah Pradesh, India. In the course of his visit, he invited me to come to India the following winter and conduct a series of meetings with him. I had never sensed any call from God to do overseas ministry. But, mostly to be courteous to my Indian brother, I said, "OK, let's pray and ask God about it." We got on our knees in my office. As we prayed, I felt my heart completely change. I began weeping and sensed a clear call to travel halfway around the earth. Bose was thrilled. Cathy was too. She was ever the consummate "helper suitable" (Genesis 2:18) to me. We started making plans. I prepared messages. We shared our trip with the body, and they graciously contributed $10,000 to fund the mission. We recruited our twin sons Peter and Andrew, who were high school seniors at the time, to go with us as videographers and good will ambassadors. Everything came together, and we were scheduled to depart the first week of January 1995. Everything, I say, except our visas.

When I had filled out the paperwork for the Indian visa, I had stated my purpose was "evangelistic ministry"—a definite no-no, I learned later. I was supposed to say "tourist." Because evangelistic ministry by foreigners is officially illegal in India, they were holding up our visas. Our bags were packed. It was the early morning of the day we were to fly out of San Francisco around midnight. I was going to have to cancel the whole trip if we didn't have the official entry stamps in our passports. So I got on the phone with the Indian Embassy in San Francisco, and the man on the line said, "Okee Mr. Kingham. I'll see vat vee can do."

My family and some friends were all there holding their breath and praying. He called back and said, "Okee, Mr. Kingham, since you are a holy man, vee have worked out a vay for you to get your visas. Come to the embassy, and vee vill help you."

So I grabbed Bethany who was home from college for the Christmas break, and we jumped into our Jeep Cherokee and drove the two hours to San Francisco. We found the embassy. Bethany sat down in the waiting area as I went in to meet with the ambassador. He smiled broadly and said, "Vee have vorked out a vay for you to receive your visas. Simply take this piece of paper and write, 'I vill not engage in any religious evangelistic activities vile in India.' And sign your name."

He was asking me to lie. I was caught in a trap. I stared at the blank paper as I talked with God in my heart. The plane was leaving tonight. We had three weeks of meetings scheduled in three cities in Andrah Pradesh. Just then, my ambassador host excused himself to go attend to a phone call. I was left alone staring at the paper. I clearly remember the moment when I said to God, "I will not build my ministry in India on a lie."

My ambassador friend returned. He looked at my paper, and I said, "I'm sorry, sir, but I can't lie. We're going to your country to work with my Indian friend and share the gospel of Jesus with your people."

He smiled, and asked me for my passports. So I slid the pile of four passports across to his side. I was not sure what he was doing. But he began vigorously turning the pages, stamping each one, and scribbling something. As he did, he asked me where we were going to be travelling. I told him. Then he gathered up the pile of passports, handed them to me with a big grin and said, "Enjoy your trip to my country."

He had given us the visas! I hugged the passports as I ran out, thinking he might change his mind if I hung around. I was a hundred feet down the street when I heard Bethany's voice, "Dad!" In my rush to get out of there, I had totally forgotten she was there. So we rejoiced together as we drove back to Woodland. That miracle became a huge touchstone which proved crucial in keeping us going as soon as we got to India.

It was a long journey half-way around the earth. I preached my first two services (morning and evening) to the people of Bose's hometown, Vijayawada. I had never preached with an interpreter, and I kept losing my place as I waited for him to finish. (It was apparent that he was greatly amplifying and embellishing what I said.) I was still feeling the effects of jet lag. The audience was not what Bose had promised. I had a message for unbelievers; they were all from his church. I struggled to communicate with those dear people. Afterwards, as we talked with our hosts, we found out that the people were not impressed with me at all. In fact, they were asking him, "Why did you bring this man over here?"

I remember lying wide awake in the middle of the night (we were still jet-lagging) and talking with Cathy. We were grossed out by many of the sights and smells of India. We had rats running over our bed in the dark. The people didn't want us here. Should we just change our flight and go home? But that miracle at the embassy just days before kept reminding us that God obviously wanted us to be there. So we had a serious time of prayer asking God for strength to press through the hardships and love the people. We asked Him to bear fruit which would obviously be from Him.

Things started to change the next day. The people warmed up to us. They began to respond to Bose and me as we team-preached in two languages. We had the joyful privilege of seeing several of them baptized in the Ganges River right next to Hindu phallic images. By the time we were leaving they wanted to accompany us on a long six-hour drive to the airport. God totally turned things around and used us to bless scores of people with the gospel. It was a blessing to link up with our brothers and sisters from such a different culture, but it was also a powerful lesson about staying the course in the face of discouragement and opposition. And God showed us His tender watch care on our final journey of that India adventure. Several of the Indians had become great friends and wanted to see us back to the airport. We were originally booked on a train between Tirupati and the airport in Madras. But when the others wanted to join us, Bose rented a large van, and we drove the six hours. About midway on our trip, we came upon a huge head-on train-wreck on the very tracks which we would have been travelling on. It was horrific. One of those trains shouldn't have been on the track at that moment. And we could have faced that same oncoming train if we hadn't changed our plans. India did more than stamp visas in my passport. It dramatically shaped my love for people of a very different culture, and it opened a window of God's provision and protection which I could have never seen any other way. Thanks, Bose, for inviting us.

We often don't realize the depth of influence people have on us until they're gone. That was certainly true in the case of my dad. He passed away in the fall of 1998, and it was, to be sure, an emotionally wrenching loss. But I was busy with ministry and caring for my mom. So it wasn't until about a year later that I was suddenly and unexpectedly exposed to the wound still bleeding in my soul. I have related the following story in my previous book, but it bears retelling here.

I needed to do some plumbing repair in the upstairs attic of our home. The work required me to turn off the water on the ground level, climb a flight of stairs, climb a ladder into the crawl space of the attic, and then crawl on my belly through the dusty insulation to the place where the pipes were located. I am not a skilled plumber, and so the project took the usual three trips to the supply store while the water was turned off to the house. I made many trips up and down, and each time I was rubbing more dust off of the ceiling joists. On the final triumphant trip when I turned on the water and returned to find my repair was not leaking, I suddenly saw something which immediately jarred my mind and instantly opened a fountain of tears to flow from my eyes. My travels across the joists had uncovered a board with a single word on it scrawled with a carpenter's keel (like blue crayon). It was my dad's unmistakable handwriting, and it said, "Pattern."

Before my conscious mind could unravel what was happening, I was deeply emoting and feeling the pain of my father's loss. He had helped me build that part of the house nearly twenty years before. He had cut the rafters by making copies of a pattern rafter. Evidently we made one too many rafters, and the pattern rafter didn't get used, so it went into bracing the ceiling joists.

There it was: my dad's life, yanked up from my memory by the sudden sight of the word "pattern." I lay there in the attic for about five minutes just weeping and feeling the power of his remembered presence. As the emotions calmed, I began realizing my dad had been the pattern for so many aspects of my life—and now God was telling me it was my turn to be the pattern to others whom He would be placing in my path. This experience was an early harbinger of what God would show me during my sabbatical about four years later.

When the calendar turned to the new millennium, I had been ministering at WBC for twenty-two years. The ministry had matured and become strong. What we planted in 1978 was now a fixture in the community. My kids had grown and were all living away from our home. I was a grandpa (Tyler, our oldest grandchild was born in 1997). Jonathan had served five years in the Navy. Bethany was in grad school for her teaching credential. Peter and Andrew were finishing their undergraduate studies. My father, as I said, had been called home to glory from heart disease at age eighty-two, and my sister and I were attending to the care of our mother who was deep into Alzheimer's. We had come to Woodland to live by faith. But now, twenty-two years later, most of what we were doing was rather ordinary and didn't seem to require much faith at all.

12

Oroville—New Horizons

I remember the day when I realized a subtle—but serious—change had happened in my life at WBC. I was in the foyer before the service started, and families were arriving at the front door. As they passed me, the little kids politely looked up and said, "Good morning, Pastor Ron." From their standpoint, it was entirely appropriate. It was reverential respect for the "man of God." But for me it was a sign that things were different.

We weren't the rag-tag bunch of iconoclasts who had gathered in the Women's Clubhouse in 1978. We were a respectable church, much like the other respectable churches I had broken away from. We had developed a church culture which was starting to slip away from the informality and freshness of the early church which I so loved and appreciated. I had repeatedly told people *not* to call me Pastor Ron. I would say: "I don't call you Painter John or Nurse Nancy. Just call me Ron. I just happen to have a pastoral teaching job here at the church, but I'm just one of you."

I had intentionally kept my college and seminary sheepskins off the wall of my study so as not to set up a clergy-laity divide (which in my opinion is unbiblical, see Matthew 23:8-11). I think many people at WBC had no idea I was a graduate of "prestigious" Dallas Theological Seminary. I worked hard to keep the playing field level, but the tide was starting to push back and force me into a more traditional role. It caused Cathy and me to start having serious talks about whether our days in Woodland were over.

As we talked and prayed, God started showing me several reasons why I was finished in Woodland. One day I was in the midst of a counseling session with a woman who was—well, to put it bluntly—being stupid and selfish and wanting me to side with her in her foolishness. I lost my cool. I shouted a disrespectful word to her. And then I had to immediately ask for forgiveness. But it opened a window into my weary heart. It showed me I was exhausted in my role as a counselor. When I probed the matter privately with the Lord, He showed me I had lost my patience with people who know God's truth and yet blatantly reject it and then expect me to feel bad for them when they reap the consequence of their own poor choices. I knew this was unChrist-like, and I needed some space and time to heal and recover.

As I continued this time of self-evaluation, I also saw that I was receiving a regular paycheck like clockwork. There were no more challenges to my income. We were doing fine, and I seldom thought about asking God for my daily bread. In addition, I took an honest look around the congregation. They were looking a little long in the tooth and gray in the head—just like me. It is a common occurrence for church congregations to resemble the age of their shepherd. We tend to be most credible to our peers. But I knew this was an unhealthy sign. I was not connecting well with the younger generation. WBC needed some young blood. So as Cathy and I weighed these converging factors, we became convinced that our season of ministry in Woodland was coming to an end. I shared my decision with the elders, and we prayerfully began strategizing my exit. I agreed to stay as long as it took them to find a new shepherd for the flock. During this season of transition, Cathy and I (along with my sister Judy) were caring for precious Mom. We had her in a wonderful residential care facility about five blocks from our house. God mercifully allowed her disease to progress very quickly. From the time we assumed her care until God called her home was less than three years. She passed away in February 2002, and with her passing, we felt our remaining ties to Woodland being severed. So we made our official announcement to the church body that we would be leaving.

I remember the day I finished my sermon with, "Before we're dismissed today, I have an important message to share with you." Then I read a carefully worded letter to the flock which encapsulated our decision and the basic strategy the elders would be using to find my replacement. I finished the letter, and the audience sat in stunned silence. No one moved for several moments. In the quiet you could hear the sound of sobbing. Their beloved shepherd of twenty-three years was leaving them. A good number of them had never known any other shepherd than me. It was emotional for me as well. I loved them and they loved me. But God had shown me I must leave, and that required moving through the time of shock and grief.

It took the Search Committee nearly eighteen months to find the man they believed God was sending to WBC. I was sorry they had to look far away. I had hoped for a long time I would be able to disciple and groom the man who would succeed me right there in the context of WBC, and he would be an extension of my personal call and vision, and he would know the people well. But no such man was to be found. So the committee searched far and wide for the new pastor-teacher. In July 2003, we installed the new leader, Verl Taylor, a fellow alum from DTS, and most recently of Texas. He and his wife Daisy shouldered the leadership for the next seventeen years. I would like to say that Verl shared my vision, but it became apparent to me that he held a more traditional view of church, and over time the church slowly morphed away from its roots. I prayed often for him and for the people I loved so much, but on those occasions when I re-visited WBC as the "former pastor," it wasn't the same. Most of the people whom I partnered with during my twenty-four years there had left, sensing the shift away from the founding ethos. God still loves those precious people in Woodland, and I pray that what they learned and experienced during those exciting body life days of WBC will never fade from their memories.

Cathy and I needed a rest. We had absolutely no idea what God had for us next. I was fifty-six and still in good health, although I had had a serious brush with my mortality a couple years before. I had heeded the doctor's directives and lost weight, changed my diet, and started exercising. With the passing of both of my parents, my sister and I had received a moderate inheritance, and (for the first time in our adult lives) we had money to fund a time of transition. So we planned a sabbatical at R-Wild Horse Ranch, west of Red Bluff, California.

We had bought into the ranch in 1991, shortly after our Yosemite cabin burned. For more than a decade, the ranch had been a wonderful place for us to get away. I would go there for solitude and wildflower photoshoots. We would take small groups with us. And I was able to hold WBC men's retreats of sixty to seventy men there several times. We loved the ranch, and as owners, we could essentially live at the ranch free. Cathy found a spacious used thirty-foot fifth wheel which we bought, along with a big Ford F-250 pickup to pull it. After finishing the summer at Bethany's wedding in southern California and then visiting son Pete in Durango, Colorado (where he was doing conservation and trail work), we pulled the fifth wheel up to the ranch and parked it. A dear friend from WBC, Rachel Burt, needed housing, and so she moved into our Woodland home, and we settled in for the fall and winter at the ranch in our trailer. Cathy continued to work her four-on, ten-off schedule at the hospital in Woodland, so she would travel back and forth, staying with Rachel while in Woodland.

Our sabbatical was a marvelous hinge of transition in our lives. In addition to the basic job of resting and allowing our weary minds and bodies to be restored, I had two serious objectives: (1) work on listening to God and discerning what He had for us in this new era of our lives, and (2) start writing the book about the Lord's Table which had been stirring in my heart for years. I would often take my folding chair out under the shade of a spreading manzanita bush and spend a couple hours with my Bible open just taking in the Word and asking God to speak to me. Over and over I would ask Him, "Lord, *who am I* now that I'm fifty-six and have finished my assignment in Woodland? And *what do you want me to do* as I run the final laps of my earthly race?" And for many days, I would hear nothing from the Lord. Then I would switch gears and work on research for my book. This was before the internet had caught hold, so Cathy and I would visit the libraries in Redding and Red Bluff and bring books back to the ranch to read. It was a God-ordained time of refreshment and recharging for the next stage of our journey.

For some reason, God has chosen to speak with me several times when I'm fully engrossed in worship. One Sunday sometime around Christmas, we were back in Woodland for a short visit home. We attended worship at WBC, and the music was particularly uplifting. I was pouring out my heart of love to God, and I suddenly heard Him say, "Ron, you're a raven."

I immediately knew what it meant. The Old Testament prophet Elijah had been cared for by ravens, and God told me that my calling in this latter stage of my life was to pour myself into feeding younger servants, His Elijahs, who are on the front line of the spiritual battle. In the days which followed, Cathy and I talked at length about what it meant. I began to search for places where a raven could find his Elijahs. I prepared a resumé and sent it out to various nearby Christian colleges. We mostly hung out at the ranch, and I intensified my efforts on researching and writing the book. But the Lord had shown me I was a raven, and I started to itch to meet my Elijahs. Now my daily prayer had changed to "Lord, when is this sabbatical over? When do I get going as a raven?"

Well, I was back in Woodland on a weekend in February, again deeply immersed in worship on a Sunday morning. I was stunned as I heard the voice of God loudly say to me, "Ron, the sabbatical is over when I give you a song."

I poked Cathy sitting next to me, and said, "You're not going to believe what the Lord just said to me. I'll tell you after the service." So over lunch I explained my utter amazement that God was going to give me a song as the finish line of the sabbatical. It was inconceivable because I had never in my life—as much as I had tried—been able to write a song. Most of my children were songwriters. I would ask them, "Where does the tune come from?"

They would say incomprehensible things like, "The guitar writes the song," or "It just starts flowing into my mind." Well, a song had never come flowing into my mind like that, and I knew if I got a song, it would truly be a supernatural thing.

During my sabbatical, I had been having sweet communion with the Lord in my daily Quiet Time. A few weeks back I had begun reading and meditating in the book of 2 Corinthians. It had really been connecting with my pregnant soul. For about three weeks, I had been "stuck" in chapters 3, 4, and 5. Every day I went back over the same passage, and God kept showing me new insights which were very poignant to me at this transition season of my life. It was Monday morning, the day after God had emphatically told me He would terminate the sabbatical with a song. I opened my Bible to 2 Corinthians 3 again and began soaking in the message. Before long the thoughts in that passage started to echo in my head, and I found myself singing a song. It went on for a few moments, and then suddenly I stopped and asked myself, "*What song is that? I've never heard that song before!*" And like a bolt of lightning, I was overwhelmed with tears as I realized God was downloading the song right at that moment. I ran in to tell Cathy, and we rejoiced together for a moment. Then I quickly returned to start writing it all down before I forgot it. In about an hour, it was complete, and so was the sabbatical. The song was entitled "This Earthen Vessel," and some weeks later, I had the joy of hearing it sung by a mixed quartet for a worship service at WBC.

So from that day, we began making plans to leave. I had told Verl Taylor it would not be fair to him to have me nearby, so I began sprucing up the Woodland house to get it ready for sale. Within days of the "the song," I got a phone call from William Jessup University in Rocklin inviting me to join their faculty as a part-time adjunct professor in the Christian Leadership track of the Degree Completion Program. The students were hungry young adults who had dropped out of college but were now returning to complete their B.A. It was a perfect fit for this raven, because they wanted me to be a "cohort mentor" which meant I would teach several classes to the same group and act as a mentor and shepherd to guide them into places of ministry in the kingdom.

The only thing that remained to be figured out was where we would live. Cathy and I prayed fervently, and we discerned that we needed to land somewhere within driving distance of both Rocklin and Woodland. Cathy wanted to continue working as an RN. Her employment was doubly important: she would provide a stable financial anchor while I fixed a place for us to live, and she wanted to continue the wonderful niche of ministry she had carved out both to the patients and the staff of the hospital. She was flourishing as a psych nurse. Her four-on, ten-off schedule became a wonderful asset for us for the next decade. She would travel to Woodland, stay with our dear friends, and work her four-day shift. Then she would be by my side in our ministries and projects for the next ten days. Her pay was enough to completely support us. My teaching at Wm. Jessup paid very little. I saw it as a raven ministry.

So with our two anchor points in mind, we began making search trips all over the hills to the east of us. It was largely discouraging. Either the areas were too crowded and expensive, such as the area around Auburn and Grass Valley. Or if they were affordable, they were too remote and disconnected from social life. I was engaged in writing my book and prepping the house for sale. One day, sometime in early April 2003, Cathy came up to talk with me at my desk where I had been hunkered down in front of the computer writing all day. I evidently looked bedraggled. She pronounced,

"You *need* to get away, Ron. Let's go on another property search outing."

I agreed. Since I had exhausted most of the places I already knew about, I suggested, "Let's go up towards Lake Oroville. I've passed by there many times on fishing trips, but I've never looked around the area."

So the next day we drove to Oroville. As we approached, we were not impressed with what we saw. Oroville does not wear its dress-up clothes along the roads coming into town. But it is a gorgeous place in the Sierra foothills of northern California. We stopped at the office of a realtor who gave us a bunch of listings. After a couple hours (I believe it was God's guidance), we found another sleeper, a piece of land which had been overlooked for years because of the steep hill leading up to it and the thick foliage that obscured its awesome view. It was wildflower season, and the place was aflame with God's botanical beauty. I called Nathan, and a couple days later he came up and scoped it out with us. He climbed up in an oak tree and announced, "Dad, I think it has a view."

Then I asked, "What do you think about us buying this?"

He wisely replied, "It's a *huge* project, Dad. You know that, don't you?"

I nodded, "Yes, but I have a huge God to help me."

So Cathy and I presented it to the Lord. He gave us the green light, so we offered $63,000, and the sellers accepted our offer. The last piece of our transitional puzzle was in place, and we were the proud (and a little scared) owners of seven and a half acres at 70 Harry Lane, Oroville, California, later to be dubbed Stonehaven. Our original plan was to buy an existing house and perhaps modify and update it to suit our needs. But this was an all-out development project which would require clearing the land, putting in a well and septic system, designing the house, and then building it. But I had the miracle-working Lord to guide me and four healthy strong sons to lend their brains and brawn.

I helped Cathy dodge poison oak as we walked out on the property. Cathy was not immune like me. The immunity I had developed in high school was going to become a very wonderful asset on this land! The place was ablaze with three different varieties of poison oak! We held a little dedication service that day in early April 2003. "Lord, we want this property to become a place of blessing to us and many others, including our precious family. Give us the wisdom and strength to do this monstrous project."

God created me as a visionary with a supernatural ability to see the final product of an undertaking in my mind's eye. It was that way with the skating rink in Woodland, and it was that way with this new adventure. I could picture wonderful things happening right around me. We returned to Woodland with a gleam in our eyes and a spring in our step. We put our home up for sale, and in about two months, we were able to find a solid buyer (without a realtor... again), and we got a remarkably high price, as the market was rising in the summer of 2003. The cash we received from our Woodland home enabled us to build and occupy our new home without a mortgage. I am still amazed by that!

We had a big moving-day party, and a dozen of our friends came to help us pack up our life's "things" into a big truck and a trailer. We hauled it all to a storage place in Oroville. We said goodbye to Woodland and all our dear friends, hitched up the fifth wheel and moved it to a mobile home park in Oroville. We settled into our new life in a strange town where we didn't know one soul. But we only lived in the fifth wheel for two months.

We quickly realized we were trapped in the fifth wheel. We couldn't entertain guests or family, and I had no place for my tools for the development project. So Cathy searched for a little house in town. She found a perfect little three-bedroom-one-bath on a happy corner on the northern edge of Oroville (technically called Thermalito). That great little house served as our base of operation for the two years of the building of Stonehaven. I spent about two days a week preparing lessons and grading papers for my weekly evening classes at Wm. Jessup. Cathy continued her cyclical work at the hospital, and I spent the rest of my time starting to clear the land and conceive a design for a home on the property.

As I slowly cleared the dead trees and brush, we began to see more and more of the unique beauty of our new gem. An eye-popping view of the Sutter Buttes, called the smallest mountain range in the world, began to emerge, so we started envisioning a home which would incorporate that view into its personality. The land was also graced with a plethora of granite rock outcroppings of various configurations and sizes. We wanted to feature them in our plans. Cathy searched through a pile of architectural design books and found an idea which seemed like it would work on the property. From the air it looked like a jet plane with wings coming off at angles on both sides (following the contours of the rock outcroppings) and the fuselage pointed at the view of the Sutter Buttes.

We started visiting a number of existing churches in town on Sundays, and on our one Sunday to visit the Nazarene church, a couple named Doug and Yvonne French invited us to join them for lunch. If I recall correctly, it was the only time anyone ever invited us to lunch during our years in Oroville. It was obviously a divine appointment. They just happened to know a good architect—their son-in-law, Cash Colby. We contacted Cash that week, and he undertook the task of translating Cathy's basic idea of the jet plane into plans which I could build from. (Cash Colby became a valuable resource for me, since I didn't have *any* construction connections in Oroville.) Cathy drove the design process. After all, it was her nesting place. I had only two requests: I wanted open exposed trusses in the fuselage/great room (I have always loved open trusses), and I wanted the angle of the wings to be 30°. I remembered from my days in high school geometry that the hypotenuse of a 30°-60°-90° right triangle is half the length of the base leg. I am so glad I specified that angle!! Without that, cutting all the angles during the framing would have been a total nightmare.

It was a joy to teach at Wm. Jessup, especially in those early days. My students were avid learners, and they were looking for guidance as they pursued their role in furthering Jesus' kingdom. They were my Elijahs, and God supernaturally enabled this raven—the morning person who falls asleep so early—to be fully alive and awake until I arrived home around midnight (the classes met once a week from 6:00 PM to 10:00 PM). I still marvel at the way God miraculously energized me to teach night classes. Teaching in the academic arena was quite an adjustment for me. In my prior thirty years of teaching within the context of the gathered church community, I strove hard to remain a peer nudging peers. But the moment I stood in the college classroom, I was perceived as the expert, the one with the answers. My students were paying big bucks to learn from "the master." It caught me off guard at first. But God graciously enabled me to find a path through the potentially lethal ego-puffing minefield. Through my personal involvement with each of them as their "cohort mentor," through my servant-heart in the classroom, in my comments on their papers, and through my personal stories of my own weaknesses which had been transformed by Jesus, the Lord helped me establish a healthy professor/student balance. So for the better part of seven years, I taught one—and occasionally two—classes per week at Wm. Jessup. I am humbled that God used me powerfully to feed and inspire a terrific group of young Christian leaders. I vacated my post when the college made a major change in the curriculum, dropping many of the classes which I loved teaching.

Through the fall and winter of 2003-2004, we worked on clearing the property, drilling an extremely reliable and productive water well, getting plans drawn, applying for a building permit, and gathering resources for the big project. The building of Stonehaven is a litany of stories of God's miraculous intervention helping me do a project which was, quite frankly, way over my head. One of the first was when He connected me with Tony Anthony. Just as we were moving to Oroville, I discovered that one of my cousins, with whom I had not been in contact for decades, was living east of Oroville. So when we got settled in our fifth wheel, I told Cathy I wanted to look up my long lost cousin Jan. We paid a visit to her and her husband Tony, whom I had never met. It turned out that their place was only a couple miles farther up the hill from our new property. They had also recently located here after Tony retired from construction. He just "happened" to have bought both a bulldozer and a backhoe to build his own place, and he just "happened" to offer his equipment and skills as an operator for our project. Suffice it to say that Cousin Tony became an invaluable resource in the early days of developing

Stonehaven. He began digging rocks and stumps in April 2004, preparing the pad for the house.

The next moment of supernatural help came the day I tried to lay out the house. I spent most of a day attempting to establish the corners of the house from the dimensions on the plans. But I couldn't get the rooms to square up. I despaired of ever getting this project off the ground. I went home that night quite discouraged. I prayed, "Lord, help!"

And He said, "Remember your geometry and your trigonometry."

I was immediately catapulted back to my days as an engineer. I started drawing triangles (thank God for the 30° design) and calculating distances from a set of reference lines which I could easily stake out on the property. The next day, the layout was a piece of cake. Everything checked out square.

Tony came with his backhoe and started digging the footings after I finished the layout. He taught me how to operate the bulldozer, and I was moving stumps into a pile while he was excavating for the foundation. At one point, he jumped off his rig and came over to me and announced, "Come over here. We've got a problem."

He was digging the trench for the part of the foundation which would support one of the front corners of the great room. He had encountered a huge rock in the middle of the ditch. It was five feet in diameter near the surface of the ground and three times that size six feet deep into the ground. "We're not moving that rock," Tony quipped.

So with my new "cell phone," I dialed up Jim Pursell, the engineer who had signed the plans, asking him what we should do. He replied, "Build on that rock. The rest of the house may fall down, but that part will remain standing."

He gave me instructions on how to tie the steel right into the rock and run the stem wall right over the top of it. When I got home that night and told Cathy about it, it started to dawn on me what had just happened. Psalm 118:22-23 is a marvelous prophecy about Jesus. It reads: "The stone which the builders rejected has become the chief corner stone. This is the LORD'S doing; it is marvelous in our eyes" (NASB). It harkens back to an incident which occurred during the building of Solomon's Temple. And it points forward to the bittersweet reality that the Jewish leaders rejected Jesus while God was exalting Him to the place of the risen King of Kings and Lord of Lords. Many times during the next fourteen years I had the joy of showing visitors to Stonehaven how it was founded on the rock which the builders rejected. To me, that rock became symbolic of my life. I had almost rejected Him back in 1966, but instead, He became the unshakable foundation of all my life that followed. How many people do you know who have such a testimony to their faith exhibited in the very foundation of their house?

During the framing stage of Stonehaven, I was able to employ the help of two young men from the church in Woodland who were freshly out of high school, Jared Bunch and Darren Draper. They came and lived in our vacant fifth wheel which was parked behind our little house in town. Cathy cooked for them, and they provided me the young strong help every construction project requires. They learned some basic skills, and we had opportunities to talk about God and life. They were both a great blessing. Jared came first. He helped with the dirty, "grunt" work as we built the forms for the concrete foundation stem walls and later with the siding. Darren was my partner through most of the framing.

When the day came to pour the concrete for the foundation, I knew I was going to need lots of help. Years later, I am still amazed at the way God stirred about ten people from Woodland and ten from our new church we were attending in Oroville to give up a Saturday morning in June 2004, to muscle concrete around a hot, dusty hilltop. Cathy promised them lunch. Maybe that was the draw. But at any rate, I needed every man and woman who came to help. We poured out four nine-yard trucks. I remember telling Cathy that night, "Well, we're committed. We're out of the ground."

And God had a very poignant way of keeping me going. There "happened" to be property along the highway between our little downtown house and our building project which became a symbol to me every time I started getting discouraged in the throes of the huge project. It was a concrete foundation which had been laid many years before and then abandoned. I would see it every day as I drove to our job. The words of Jesus would echo in my mind: "For which one of you, when he wants to build a tower, does not first sit down and calculate the cost to see if he has enough to complete it? Otherwise, when he has laid a foundation and is not able to finish, all who observe it begin to ridicule him, saying, 'This man began to build and was not able to finish'" (Luke 14:28-30, NASB). Many times I would pass that icon and breathe a prayer asking God to keep me going.

One of the sweet delights of building Stonehaven was the way my sons and son-in-love pitched in to help. They were all living far away, yet they made concerted efforts to periodically come help Dad. They are capable and hardworking builders, and they helped all along the way from the framing to the finish. But the day which stands out most memorably to me was Christmas Day 2004. All the family came to celebrate

Christmas with Mom and Dad. They were all there except for Bethany's and Nathan's families. They weren't coming until the next day, so the group agreed to hold off the festivities until the day after Christmas when everyone could join in. So what should we do with this day? It was unseasonably warm and dry. I told them the new house was ready for roof sheathing. They enthusiastically said, "Let's go."

So we spent Christmas sheathing all 3200 square feet of roof. I was measuring; Jon was cutting down on the ground; Peter and Andrew were nailing it all down on the roof. It was a thrill to see the project take such a dramatic leap forward. But it was even more fulfilling to see my sons enjoying the project with me. It made me quite proud of my boys!

Another moment where we saw God step in and help us quite dramatically was the day the roof trusses were delivered. Harry Lane, the road leading up to Stonehaven at that time was a rutted, steep, dirt road with a tight 100° turn midway up (it gained one-hundred feet in elevation from Hurleton Road up to the new house). Later we improved it and paved it. But at this time, it was a dreadfully difficult road for large vehicles to navigate. I built the open trusses for the great room, and they were stacked up on site, needing to be hoisted up by a crane. The standard trusses were built in a factory in Chico. They were loaded onto a long trailer pulled by a semi-tractor with an attached crane. The day came for the delivery. The semi started up Harry Lane and couldn't make the turn. Then I had to watch as the driver painstakingly, inch by inch, backed the huge rig down to the bottom. A less skilled driver could have tumbled down the hill in a huge mess, but he made it. Now, what were we to do? My roof was on that trailer. I prayed, and sent the driver back to Chico, telling him I needed to ask God for a plan. I went home, and Cathy joined me asking God for wisdom. At moments like that, you're tempted to think, "Why did I ever start this project? How am I ever going to finish it?"

Next morning when I got up, an idea stirred in my mind. I thought, *"We've had several deliveries of lumber to the job site, and the bobtail lumber trucks have been able to negotiate the turn on Harry Lane."* So I called the lumber company and asked them if they would rent me one of their trucks along with the driver for the day. I was told their insurance didn't allow them to do that. I silently prayed as I explained my predicament.

Then the lumber guy said, "OK, you've been a good customer. I'll help you out. I'll send out the driver who knows your road. I'll have to do it for free, though—I'm not allowed to charge you."

Whew! Now will it work? So I gathered my team of volunteers who were going to help me place the great room trusses. The factory-built trusses arrived from Chico… again, only this time they were off-loaded by the crane onto the lumber truck. It took about four loads, but we got them all up the hill! I shouted "Halleluiah" more than once that day! The crane would follow each load and hoist them to the roof. Then the crane lifted each of my trusses, and my crew of volunteers installed them. I have wondered many times since what might have happened if that lumber company had not been willing to go out on a limb for us. God was doubly gracious in giving me the idea, and in touching that lumber man to take the risk.

Yet again, I saw God answer my desperate cry for help when it came time to install the log siding in the six gables of the house. Cathy and I had decided to add a little "mountain cabin" flair to our exterior décor with half logs from a mill in Chico. So I bought $6,000 worth of beautiful half-logs. They were sitting drying in the garage at Stonehaven. The day came when it was time to start installing them, and I suddenly realized I had no idea how I was going to cut them. The logs were approximately ten inches wide by nearly four inches thick at the center. To fit into the gable, they needed to have a twenty-two-inch-long cut on each end at 23°. I went to the tool store to see if they had such a saw. They didn't. And then I looked in the tool catalogue. Still no such saw. So I cried out in my desperation, "Lord, help! What do I do?"

I went to sleep that night with the dilemma weighing heavily on my mind. I was awakened in the middle of the night, with a solution stirring in my head. I had a vision of an enormous miter box large enough to receive the huge logs. Next day, I ordered a jumbo skilsaw large enough to cut through four-inch material. And I assembled a huge miter box made of 2"x12"s and 2"x8"s. I added a piece of flat steel, which was left over from framing the walls, as a guide for the huge skilsaw to cut the precise 23° angle. It took two men to move the miter box around. Jared and I used that huge "answer to prayer" to cut all the logs for all the gables. It was a sad day when I had to dismantle it.

Perhaps the most stunning and miraculous answer to prayer came the day the cabinets were being delivered. They were assembled in a factory somewhere far away and brought to Stonehaven on a huge truck. It was the last week of December 2005. I had called the delivery company multiple times instructing them to make their delivery in a bobtail truck (remember the truss story). I had told them repeatedly, "Do not try to deliver with a semi and a trailer. We will both regret it if you do."

Well, of course, when the day came, the truck (which was supposed to arrive in the late morning) arrived in the late afternoon—and just as in my greatest fears—it was a semi with a long trailer. I stopped the driver at the bottom of the hill and told him not to go up there. He said, "Let me walk up and check it out." So he did. After looking it over, he concluded it was doable. I kept telling him he would regret it if he got stuck at the corner. But he really wanted that load off his truck. So he started up Harry Lane.

He got to the turn (which was a steep incline and a tight bend to the left of about 100°, as I said) and started spinning his huge wheels. The truck was bucking, and it started to slide on the wet dirt towards the cliff. I shouted to him to stop. Then we got out and assessed the situation. The road was now blocked. I had three neighbors who were trapped. I knew this driver was not as skilled as the truss truck driver, so I didn't even suggest trying to back down. The sun was dipping low in the sky. My cabinets were five hundred feet from their destination, but they might as well have been five hundred miles. I could envision the huge van rolling down the steep precipice on the side of the road. So I told the driver to "chill." I needed to call Cathy and have her pray with me for wisdom. She prayed with me over the phone. I got off the phone, and a crazy idea popped into my head. My next door neighbor had his own separate road which went up the hill, and there was a locked gate on the flat between my property and his. Could we possibly get a heavy duty tow truck up his driveway, across the muddy upper part of my place, set it up on Harry Lane with a winch, and then tow the semi up the hill? I honestly didn't know if the semi would just pull the tow truck *down* the mountain, or if the tow truck would have the strength to pull the semi *up* the mountain.

Having learned at this point in my life that God answers me when I pray, I said, "Let's give it a shot."

So I dialed up the towing company. They had a big truck available with a heavy duty winch. I talked with my neighbor and he graciously gave me permission to use his driveway, and he unlocked the gate. In about a half hour, the tow truck was there, and I jumped into the cab to show him where to go. My major concern was the ground near the gate. It had been raining quite heavily, and I could see me getting two trucks stuck on my property. I encouraged the driver to get a run at it. He did, and thank the Lord, we made it over to Harry Lane. He backed down the relatively flat portion of Harry Lane to the place where the road dipped downward steeply. He set up his rig at the top of the hill about two hundred feet above the stranded semi below. We placed large chock-rocks against his rear wheels. Between the two trucks, Harry Lane makes a gentle S, so it was impossible to extend the winch cable straight down to the semi. And even if we could, it would have pulled the semi right into the embankment at the turn.

At this point the story becomes incredibly supernatural. By the time the tow rig got all set up, it was pitch dark. We were working with flashlights. I asked the tow truck guy if he had some loose tow chains and pulley-blocks. Happily, he did. So I started searching with my flashlight for places to anchor the pulley-blocks. And it was at that moment I began to grasp the magnificent, gracious foreknowledge of God which was being poured out on our behalf. There just "happened" to be two giant pines (one about thirty inches in diameter and the other about forty-two inches) placed in absolutely *the* perfect locations to anchor pulley-blocks. God had planted those trees about a hundred years earlier, and they were quietly waiting there to assist in this crisis moment of rescue. With chains and pulley-blocks in hand, I dove into the wet poison oak (everything was drenched from recent rains) surrounding the big trees while one of the other men held the flashlight. I secured the pulley-blocks, and we began to thread the winch cable in a Z pattern down the hill to the semi. After hooking up to the frame of the semi, we tightened the slack.

Ray Stedman tells of an old sea captain who described the fright experienced by sailors out at sea during a particularly horrible storm. The captain quipped, "God heard from many strangers that night."

Well, our storm had just gathered full strength. It was time for God to hear from us. We three men huddled by the tow truck, and I told them I would like to pray, and they were more than willing to oblige. So I led a simple prayer pleading with God for safety and success. Then the tow truck driver devised a simple flashlight code which he would use to signal the semi driver: One flash—go, two flashes—stop. I carried a couple large rocks down by the driving wheels of the semi. The light flashed. Both engines began to loudly drive their machines. I was standing on the cliff side right next to the huge powered wheels of the semi—they were nearly as tall as me. I kept asking God to keep me alert if the truck started tumbling down the mountain. The semi started to buck and spin, but it gradually started moving... upwards! After about three feet, they stopped and I quickly threw a rock behind the tire. At that moment, I realized our rescue might actually work! And it kept on that way. It took about ten minutes to reach the first pulley-block. And, thank God, the trailer was sweetly making the turn without smashing into the embankment!

So with the semi wheels well chocked, we rearranged the cable to eliminate the first pulley-block. After about another ten minutes, we had lugged that heavy big rig up to the second pulley-block. Then we made a direct connection to the tow truck, and before we knew it, the semi was progressing under his own power. Our cabinets were safe! It was all over but the shouting! And let me tell you, there definitely was some shouting "Halleluiah!" that night on a damp and dark hillside east of Oroville. The big rig driver pulled into the driveway and unloaded the cabinets rather nonchalantly—as though nothing extraordinary had ever happened. But I knew differently. That story could have ended many other ways, and most of those scenarios were not happy endings. I was catapulted back in my mind's memory banks to the day in my dorm room at LeTourneau College when I asked God to show me evidence that Jesus is active and alive today.

With all the wonderful ways God worked to help me build Stonehaven, it shouldn't be surprising that He had good things in store for it in the days which followed. In the spring of 2006, Cathy and I moved in. About fifty guests from Woodland and Oroville made the trip up the hill to join us for a marvelous housewarming and service of dedication to the Lord. And it quickly became a place of true blessing! It lived up to its name. It was indeed a haven amidst the picturesque stones and oaks, for the next thirteen years. We designed it to be a place for family and friends to gather. Cathy had carefully crafted the floor plan to accommodate groups. It naturally flowed from inside to outside, so it was easy to find suitable venues for many different activities. I loved Stonehaven! Even though it required a massive amount of work to keep it up, especially when it was time to whack down weeds in the spring, I drew great energy from the house and the land. I trimmed trees and cut firewood, dug up thousands of rocks, and built wonderful rock walls and features. Once we moved to Oroville, we pretty much stopped going anywhere else for vacations because we felt like we were on vacation when we were home.

I have an overflowing storehouse of magnificent memories of my days at Stonehaven. Like sipping hot tea as Cathy and I sat by the wood stove on a cold clear winter day playing Upwords and basking in the view of the Sutter Buttes thirty-five miles away. Or watching a flock of wild turkeys strut their mating ritual outside our front window. Or cornhole tournaments with my entire family out on the lower terrace. Or small groups of fellow believers sitting around the great room sharing prayer and scripture together. Or celebrating our fortieth anniversary with our family and a hundred other guests out on the green terrace below the house. Or sharing a family outing with the families of my cohort of students at Wm. Jessup University. Or working with my son Peter while he taught me how to build rock retaining walls with the "pinch and lean" method of dry rock masonry. Or Thanksgiving and Christmas dinners with the family gathered around the pool-table-turned-dining-table. As I said, the memories are endless.

I have yet to tell the story of Cathy's epic battle with cancer (that's coming in Chapter 13). It was all played out at Stonehaven, and it gave rise to probably the most potent and deeply etched memory I have of my years there. Our family had learned that the cancer in their mom and "Noni" had reached Stage Four, and they organized a marvelous family gathering in February 2015 to show their love for her. It was a love-fest of food, fun, and games, climaxing with an evening of music performed by all five of our kids. They sang and played some of Cathy's favorite songs for us in the grandeur of the Great Room with its high-ceiling and open trusses. Thank God, that stirring music was recorded, and I can play it and rekindle that grand moment whenever I need to refresh the memories.

The magic of Stonehaven mirrored the magic of Camelot. It was a supernaturally designed admixture of the scenic land, the welcoming home, and the people who passed in and out. In my years prior to Stonehaven, my house/home was simply the place I lived. But during those thirteen years in Stonehaven, my home became a fountain of spiritual life and energy to me and *many* others. If you're reading this and saying, "I don't get that," just know you had to be there.

13

Our Last Years Together

When you are an iconoclast who planted and pastored a non-traditional church for twenty-four years, a church which emphasized body life and solid Biblical exposition, it's not easy to find a church in your new town. I mentioned earlier that I tended to be a square peg in the round hole of my family because of my severe case of "morning-person-itis." Well, the same was true of my experience of church in Oroville. Cathy and I began visiting the existing churches as soon as we knew we would be living in our new community. And it was, frankly, tough. I will spare you the painful details because it doesn't align with my purposes in this book. But suffice it to say, Cathy and I agonized in prayer together many times over our church involvement during our first months in Oroville. In fact, it took us four years and three failed attempts before we landed at Oroville Church of the Nazarene. And we didn't arrive there because we agreed with the doctrine, ministry approach, leadership style, or denominationalism. We invested our lives at the Naz because God told me to. After three difficult church experiences, we were pretty discouraged. One Sunday, while Cathy was away on her four-day junket at the Woodland hospital, I was sitting out on the deck of Stonehaven crying out to the Lord about my predicament. He had made it plain I was a raven, but I had no idea how to find local "Elijahs" to minister to. I knew I was too old to start a church again. How could I use my gifts and calling to nurture the kingdom of God in Oroville? God spoke to me, quite clearly and emphatically, "Ron, let go of the things you disagree with at the Nazarene church. I can use you there if you'll give it a chance."

So the next Sunday when Cathy was home, we visited OroNaz. To my utter amazement, I found a wide open door of ministry and a large pool of energized "Elijahs" there, and so we invested our hearts and lives with the people of OroNaz for the next twelve years.

Cathy began to immediately engage with the women, and I taught classes, organized small groups, established a discipleship ministry, and even had the privilege of preaching and sharing my love for the Passover and the Shroud of Turin. I served four years as a volunteer, and then Pastor Dennis Day informed me he was putting me on the church payroll as a staff Discipleship Pastor. The pay was helpful because Cathy was no longer able to work at the hospital (she quit when she was diagnosed with cancer). My deepened connection to OroNaz rather neatly coincided with the finish of my work at Wm. Jessup. One of my greatest joys was personally mentoring several young men from the Naz whom God brought into my life.

Cathy loved life at Stonehaven as I did. She was constantly looking for ways and means to make the place more inviting and special, particularly for the growing cadre of grandchildren who were appearing in our family. She would buy things (mostly at thrift stores and garage sales), and I would assemble and deploy them. It seemed like she was always cooking up a plan for the next family gathering. She invested a great deal of time enhancing her knowledge and skills of psych nursing. She was a huge collector of books so she could be a counselor to women, with good resources at her fingertips. I fixed her up with a hands-free headset for our landline telephone, and she invested countless hours multitasking household projects while she talked eagerly with friends and family on the phone. As she grew older, she intensified her passion for mentoring younger women. And our personal times at Stonehaven deepened. We started being more intentional about spending significant time in prayer together.

Our lives took a sudden left turn in the fall of 2009. We were still riding the crest of the wave of joy which followed the wonderful celebration of our fortieth wedding anniversary that summer, and I was outside working on a special stone project which I had been wanting to do for some time—the erection of Stonehaven Light, a welcoming beacon where our driveway met Harry Lane. Cathy was in Woodland for her work at the hospital. Her recent mammogram had showed an anomaly, and she had had a follow-up biopsy. I was in the middle of mixing mortar and setting stones. My phone rang and it was Cathy. "Ron, my biopsy is positive. I have breast cancer."

I don't remember what I said, but I remember how the shock wave ran through my body. I prayed with her. When I got off the phone, I lifted my hands heavenward as I shouted to God, "I'm not ready to lose her, Lord!"

And then I sat down on a rock and wept for some time. But as I meditated out there under those gorgeous oaks, I remembered how God had been faithful to me hundreds of times before, and I gained confidence that He would strengthen me to walk this new leg of the journey. The words of Lamentations 3:19-24 comforted my mind:

"Remember my affliction and my wandering, the wormwood and bitterness. Surely my soul remembers and is bowed down within me. This I recall to my mind, therefore I have hope. The LORD'S lovingkindnesses indeed never cease, for His compassions never fail. They are new every morning; great is Your faithfulness. 'The LORD is my portion,' says my soul, 'Therefore I have hope in Him'" (NASB).

They sent Cathy home from work that day, and she never went back. And thus began our eight year battle with the vicious disease which does to the body what sin does to the soul.

Our agenda abruptly changed. Now our priority was to fight cancer. And let me tell you, Cathy was a fighter. She quickly assembled mountains of research and information. And she never stopped researching until the metastasized brain tumors stopped her. First it was two surgeries to remove the lumps in her breast. Then it was radiation. But no chemotherapy! She knew the chemo was often worse than the disease, so she refused it. Then there were five years when we both ate a vegan diet which was purported to strengthen the immune system against cancer. During those years she appeared to be cancer free, but in late 2013, she began having symptoms in her lungs and motor function which led to the discovery of metastasized lesions in the lungs and brain. When her body finally succumbed to the disease, it had also spread to her bones and liver.

So while we were fighting the disease, we also had to figure out how we were going to earn our living, since Cathy had to quit working. I was sixty-three. As I said previously, back in the early days at Woodland Bible Church, I had told the elders that I didn't want them to set aside money for my retirement. So I had nothing to draw from in a retirement fund.

In addition, I had taken advantage of an option which is no longer available from the federal Social Security system: I opted out—for all ministry-related earnings. Since I was self-employed in the early days at WBC, Social Security would have taken a huge fourteen percent bite out of my check, and I didn't feel I could afford that as I tried to raise my large family on a small income. Because I had worked at various non-ministry jobs for ten years prior to opting out, I was guaranteed the minimum Social Security income of about $450 per month. Now at sixty-three, I was three years from that minimal Social Security income, and I was finished with Wm. Jessup. What were we going to do? Cathy and I started earnestly seeking God's direction. Day after day we prayed asking Him for His guidance.

Then one day while Cathy was receiving cancer treatments, I starting thinking about what a huge piece construction had been in my life. It provided for me when I was growing up; it was my full-time occupation for four years in Santa Cruz; it supported my family through seminary; and it was a key piece of my life at Woodland. I was still strong and healthy. And it was a unique moment of economic opportunity. I had never seen real estate prices drop so dramatically. In fact, the market was flooded with foreclosures—many available at one third of what they had been worth a year before. Interest rates were as low as they had ever been in my lifetime. We could become real estate investors! It was as though God had created a moment in history just for us.

So we joined an investors club and started learning investing wisdom from others who were already in the business. In the meantime, Cathy, who was still recovering from her cancer treatments, became the "searcher"—she chased all over the area for potential properties. Then one day she found a sleeper. I was hesitant. Buying that property meant leveraging the equity in Stonehaven. I remember Cathy praying, "Lord, help Ron have courage to trust You and buy our first property."

Well, I did! We bought our first property in the early spring of 2010. It turned out to be a wonderful success, and it spurred us on to further ventures. Over the course of the next eight years, the Lord enabled us to buy/sell/rent about one property per year. And in the process, He helped us set up notes on the substantial equity we created in several properties. By the time I was ready to retire, that note income was in place. Along the way, three different personal friends also stepped up and volunteered to help us do deals with short term loans. In the end, I finished up absolutely debt free with a monthly income of about $3,000 from notes. Every time that money arrives in my bank account, I have a little praise session with my Lord! One of the greatest things about our investment business was that every deal was a four-way win: for the seller (they were glad to get the place off their hands), for the buyer (they were able to have a house payment less than their previous rent), for the neighborhood (we fixed up ugly houses), and for the Kinghams (we earned a fair profit)! As I mentioned above, I had left my post in Woodland partly because I was no longer living by faith. Well, the decade of property investing gave me lots of opportunity to rediscover the exciting life of faith! Great is His faithfulness!

In the midst of our lives as investors, God graciously enabled us also to be givers. The first was a gift to Habitat for Humanity. In one of our deals, we acquired a lot on the south side of Oroville which was a great candidate for a house to be built by Habitat for Humanity. Because we were so grateful for the way our business deal had worked out, we wanted to bless a needy family, so we gave the lot to Habitat.

Another gift was also a gesture of gratitude. Sometime in 2013, one of the people who had been a private lender to help fund our investment ventures, spoke to me at church and asked if I could build her a cross out at her place. She wanted to have an outdoor chapel where she could spend Quiet Time with the Lord. I told her I was so grateful for her help in my business that I would gladly build it and install it as a gift. So I did. We will revisit that cross later in this narrative....

And a third gift was simply in response to the voice of God. A seventy-three-year-old widow from church named Arlene Hendriks, who had recently joined my team of disciple-makers, approached me with a construction question. I barely knew her. Her old homestead was on a ten acre parcel in Palermo, and she sought my advice on how to put a seven hundred square foot addition onto it so she could live there in her final years on earth. It's hard for me to explain how the Lord touched me at that moment, but I became quite clearly convinced He was directing me to become her general contractor—as a gift to her. The topic of our conversation at home over dinner that evening was a bit unusual: "I sense the Lord wants me to build an addition onto Arlene's house. It will take several months, perhaps the better part of a year. It's a big project. What do you think?"

Cathy graciously responded, "I trust you, Ron. Do what the Lord tells you to do."

Thus it was that most of 2012 was spent building Arlene's addition and tying it all in to the existing place so when you approach the house you don't see an addition. Each day I would drive over to the job, I would think how unusual it was that God wanted me to give my time away on this major project. Then one morning as I was waking up and thinking about the job, God spoke to me and explained. He said, "Arlene is a *widow indeed*, and I'm giving you a chance to share in her ministry."

I knew that term from 1 Timothy 5 in the NASB. The Lord reminded me how much He cares for widows—that's how we started Woodland Bible Church. And now He was giving me a chance to lay a good foundation in my investment business by assisting a vulnerable widow who was having a significant impact on younger women in the kingdom. It was raven's work of a different sort. In the years which followed, her ministry has been unfolding like a brilliant rose! Her published work, *Treasures Out of Trauma,* is bringing lifegiving help to a multitude of younger women who have suffered pain and abuse. Her influence has spread across several western states. When God touched me in the beginning, I had no idea who she really was. I just obeyed His voice. I'm so glad I did. A huge piece of my life story is the way God has infused His care of widows into the fabric of my soul.

As soon as I finished Arlene's project, I turned my attention to finishing the book I had begun nearly a decade before. After several months of intense writing, re-writing, and editing, *Glimpses of Glory* appeared in print in the early fall of 2013. As soon as the book was finished, I prepared a traveling seminar to introduce the concepts in the book to pastors and other church leaders who wanted to enrich their gatherings around The Table. I was excited to share with anybody who would listen! But it was not to be.

Cathy was experiencing disturbing neurological symptoms which concerned her doctors. So she underwent several scans and a lung biopsy. The reports came back that the cancer had metastasized significantly to her lungs and brain. And there were some "spots" on her liver—possibly malignant. Of course, being the fighter she was, she rolled up her mental sleeves and determined to confront this enemy with the most potent weapons available. But she knew she didn't want—couldn't tolerate, more accurately—the traditional chemotherapy. She had suffered from fibromyalgia and severe headaches all her adult life and wisely realized that her immune system couldn't endure the vicious terror of chemo.

So we had some tear-stained, serious prayer times together banging on the gates of heaven as we sought God's direction about what she should do. Even though she was a trained medical professional herself, she had always leaned in the direction of more natural, holistic, functional approaches to treatment of various diseases. She began to order magazines and books, and we began reading them together. One book told encouraging stories of effective cancer treatment using novel, non-traditional methods. And it told of a clinic less than an hour away from our daughter Bethany's home in southern California. We were already scheduled to gather with most of our kids and grandkids down there for Thanksgiving at their beach house in San Clemente, so we decided to pay a visit to Dr. Jergen Winkler at his Quantum Functional Medicine (QFM) clinic in Carlsbad while we were there.

I remember that November day at the beach house on the cliff overlooking the Pacific Ocean. We sent the grandkids out while we shared with the adults only. We announced to the family that Cathy's cancer had returned, and now she was in stage four. Her days were numbered unless God intervened quite dramatically. He might be calling her home soon, but she was not ready to go yet! They all hugged her and shared their tearful love. The next day we drove to QFM and met Dr. Winkler and his wonderful staff. We were deeply impressed with the brilliant doctor, and with his attentive team. And in the course of our visit, we discovered that the doc and most of his staff loved Jesus! So we came away wanting very much for Cathy to start treatment there, but knowing it was *way* out of our league. He did not take Medicare, and we didn't have the money to fund it. We reported back to the family that we hoped to come down and start a month of treatments at the first of the year, but we had no idea how to pay for it.

Well, our precious kids grabbed the bull by the horns, and within days, thousands of dollars were pouring into an online caring account. Within a matter of about three weeks, we had the $20,000 needed for our first month of treatments! So on January 2, 2014, we commenced treatments at the QFM clinic. It was primarily infusion therapy, so Cathy had a surgical procedure to implant an IV port in her chest. Our sweet daughter Bethany (and Mark and P.J.) were incredibly gracious, and gave us a place to stay while she underwent therapy at QFM. Over the next three and a half years, we went back about six times—each time it was because precious friends gave us the money we needed for the treatments. They loved Cathy at the clinic, and Dr. Winkler and his staff bent over backwards to accommodate her. Even though she was suffering most of time, she was always the bright light in the infusion room of sick cancer patients. Often when we returned to Stonehaven, she would continue the infusion treatments at home, assisted by a dear visiting-nurse friend, Rosie Glaze, who volunteered to help Cathy.

People loved my sweet Cathy. She had been reaching out to many of them while she was strong, and now in her weakness they were reaching back to her. The brain lesions were impairing neurological functions, especially her balance, hand coordination, and reaction speed. So for the last three years of her life, she was no longer able to drive our car. At least a dozen different friends volunteered to be her chauffeurs. I was still engaged in my investment/rehabbing business, so I was often gone in the daytime. These friends would come from Oroville out to Stonehaven, pick up Cathy and take her shopping, to doctor appointments, and out to lunch. I was amazed at how many people loved Cathy! It was because she was a beautiful reflection of the love of Jesus in the midst of a miserable battle with cancer. And believe me, cancer is a *miserable* disease.

One example will help demonstrate the sweet tangible love so many people had for Cathy in her time of weakness. When one of her chauffeurs came to pick her up one day for an appointment, Cathy painfully apologized for taking her time and needing "babysitting." The dear friend chided her, "I'm not babysitting you! I'm guarding the Treasure." Cathy brightened when she realized that her friends considered it a blessing and a privilege to assist her in her weakness.

I instinctively knew that Cathy's days were numbered, and I worked hard to find ways to enhance our good memories in the midst of this ugly battle. I have wonderful memories of candlelight dinners together, games played by the woodstove, books we read together, and especially sweet times of prayer together. Our default mode was to talk about the cancer, so when it was possible, I tried to lighten up the atmosphere. Our kids were also amazing. They came to our place as much as their busy lives would permit. Seeing her precious grandkids was even better medicine than Dr. Winkler had!

I don't think many people knew how much Cathy suffered in her last years, because she was so good at rising above it and hiding it. Pain and nausea were her constant companions. The pain became excruciating toward the end when the cancer reached her bones and caused frightful cramping. She had to sleep in a recliner for the last year, and what sleep she got was fitful and intermittent. In her misery I would want to reach out and hold her to comfort her, but at my touch she would cry out in pain from her fibromyalgia. It was a horrible thing for me to watch. I saw the bitter fruit of cancer in her body, and it made me very angry that I could do nothing about it except watch, pray, and serve her in her weakness. I'm a fixer, and I couldn't fix her. (My anger at her unfixable condition exposed the grief that was churning within *me*.) But when someone would come to visit, or she would be out with friends, Cathy somehow managed to bury the pain and be sprightly. She was truly amazing.

She would tell you that she was able to rise above the pain and weakness because it was her passion to live out the truth of 2 Corinthians 12:9-10:

> "And [God] has said to me, 'My grace is sufficient for you, for power is perfected in weakness.' Most gladly, therefore, I will rather boast about my weaknesses, so that the power of Christ may dwell in me. Therefore I am well content with weaknesses, with insults, with distresses, with persecutions, with difficulties, for Christ's sake; for when I am weak, then I am strong" (NASB).

So it was that when we were asked to share our story as a sermon at OroNaz in the fall of 2016, Cathy chose that passage as our text for the message. I taught the meaning of the text, but Cathy shared how the meaning was a living reality in her life-journey with cancer. She spoke with such compelling, anointed Holy Spirit power that day! It was truly a message which had been refined in the crucible of her own experience.

Although Cathy had a hard time accepting the fact that she was declining, it was all too apparent to those of us around her. Once the brain tumors started growing, I eased into the roles which she had been carrying so capably for so long, like meal planning and cooking and house cleaning. Her life was full of efforts to fight her disease and keep in touch with all her dear family and beloved friends and younger women whom she continued to mentor. While it was incredibly hard to watch her suffer, I am grateful that God put me next to her as her servant and helper and encourager. She was called on to suffer greatly, and I had the privilege of lovingly honoring the vows I had made to her in June 1969 to "care for her in sickness or in health." And at that point, she required pretty constant care.

We received a $20,000 check from dear friends in July of 2017, and Cathy and I began planning for another round of treatments at QFM. Our plans got hurried up a bit when a horrible fire broke out in early August, threatening our home. We were forced to evacuate. As we drove through the police barricade away from Stonehaven, we stopped and had a time of prayer together. The fire was raging out of control. I prayed, "Lord, we love that place. We ask You to save it. But if You want to take it, we release it. It's just a house."

So instead of staying somewhere local, we decided to evacuate all the way to southern California. I remember sitting in a chair next to Cathy as she began her first IV bag and telling the nurses that northern California was on fire, and we weren't sure we'd ever see our home again. (Thankfully, the firefighters were able to hold the line at Forbestown Road, a half mile from Stonehaven!)

But it was quite apparent to me on that first day at the clinic that Cathy was not well. She became so sick from her first infusion treatment I had to take her in her wheelchair to the ER. The next day I broached the difficult conversation that I was seeing serious signs that God would be calling her home soon, and we both needed to get ready. It was painful for her to accept that. She was such a fighter, and she so loved life and her family and ministry! After some intense and painful prayer time together, we decided to curtail the treatments and bring her home sooner than originally planned. Just as we were getting ready to make the long drive home, I received an email from our dear friend Rachel Burt. She said she had just retired and would like to come spend a couple weeks with us taking care of Cathy for me. I was thrilled at God's gracious provision! Her help would give me a chance to organize a team of caregivers for Cathy. So we returned to Stonehaven.

Rachel arrived and was truly a Godsend. She loved Cathy and provided wonderful care and company while I worked on assembling a team of daytime caregivers. For twenty years I had been paying premiums on a long-term care insurance policy. So I had resources to fund a wonderful group of five ladies who loved Cathy. My plan was for them each to work one day a week, while I would care for Cathy at nights and on weekends. During the two weeks Rachel was there, Cathy was functional enough to have meals with us and even sit at the picnic table outside and play a game of Rummy Tiles. And during those two weeks, we made our first contact with hospice. Cathy agreed to take no further treatments to fight the cancer, and they supplied us with morphine to ease her pain.

Rachel left, and my team of caregivers began their wonderful ministry to my precious sweetheart. But my nights with her were hard. I don't function well at night, and she was miserable most of the time. More than once I had to ask my sweet partner of forty-eight years forgiveness for my brusque treatment getting her to the bathroom. The caregivers kept a care journal, and as I looked it over, it clearly documented her rapid decline. She was going fast. We weren't going to need long term care. I ordered the hospital bed from hospice and it was delivered on Friday morning.

On Thursday, I saw the Lord answer my prayer in the most dramatic way I had ever seen. As I said, nights were difficult, and I needed a better mode of communication for Cathy to call me when she needed something. So while the caregiver was watching Cathy, I drove to town to buy a better baby monitor. As I drove, I was gripped with the reality that Cathy was dying, and I knew her deep passion was to see godly older women mentoring godly younger women. I realized that this older woman was ending her journey, and I wondered how the vision would go on after she passed. I cried out quite loudly in my car, "Lord, who is going to take her torch of women's ministry?"

And that was it. I went to the store, bought the monitor and drove home. Minutes after I got home, the phone rang. It was Genessa, one of the younger women in whom Cathy had heavily invested. She said, "I know Cathy is declining. What day would be good to come and visit her?"

I looked at Cathy and said, "You'd better come right now if you want to catch her while she's still conscious." Gennesa dropped everything and came up to the house. And then I witnessed the most amazing moment. Cathy was sitting up in the recliner. Genessa walked up to her, tearfully embraced her, and then fell to her knees and said, "Cathy, I want you to know that I'm going to take the torch of your burden for women's ministry. I've been avoiding it, but the

Lord just touched me to tell you." Cathy was unable to talk, but a tear appeared in her eye. My jaw dropped. The Lord had touched Genessa at the very moment I lifted my prayer heavenward. And that was just the beginning of a phenomenal cascade of wonders that marked the passing of my precious Cathy into glory.

My kids found out Cathy was dying, and within hours, they were all there. We moved Cathy to the hospital bed (in the middle of the great room) on Friday afternoon, and by Tuesday evening she was in the presence of Jesus whom she had loved since she first entrusted her life into His hands at age sixteen. For those four days, that great room at Stonehaven became holy ground. There were always at least a half a dozen people there, sometimes many more. Dear Margie Hensley, one of the five caregivers and one of the many young women Cathy had invested in, voluntarily decided to stay there around the clock and keep watch over Cathy. It was a constant blend of music, laughter, tears, stories, memories, celebrations, scripture, and moments of somber reflection on the life of an amazing woman. People were making special trips to Stonehaven to say goodbye, and they had all been influenced by her life. I had never seen anything like it. At one point, I took leave of the great room and sat down in my study to refocus. I asked the Lord, "What is going on here?"

And very quickly, the Lord took my mind to the words of John 12:24: "Truly, truly, I say to you, unless a grain of wheat falls into the earth and dies, it remains alone; but if it dies, it bears much fruit" (NASB). He said, "Ron, Cathy is dying, but you're seeing some of the fruit her life has produced." I remember thinking how marvelous it was that she and I had chosen, many years earlier, to invest our lives in other people for the kingdom of God.

I was blessed to be standing at her bedside as my precious Cathy quietly drew her last breath of earth's air and passed sweetly into the arms of Jesus on September 12, 2017, almost eight years after first learning she had breast cancer. Only God knows, but I speculate that her herculean efforts with non-traditional medicine extended her life two or three years. In the beginning, I had not been ready to let her go, but as I watched the disease ravage her body, it gradually became easier to release her. God has His ways of peeling our fingers off the things and people we cling to too tightly. In the end, it was a privilege for me to bid her farewell as the angels carried her to glory, knowing I would see her again, this time in her glorified, disease-free body which shines like Jesus' body.

Some people were surprised that I was able to preside at her memorial service. I had been quietly grieving her loss for eight years. I was indeed bereft of my precious Cathy, but as the well-known hymn "Because He Lives" says, she had fought her final war with pain—and won! I wanted desperately to celebrate her remarkable life and her newfound freedom and deliverance from pain. It was time to rejoice. And it was a memorable memorial. Our kids sang the most beautiful music imaginable. Many people gave tribute to her investment in their lives. Jesus was honored, and it marked a glorious exclamation point on the story God had been writing in my life since a bouncy brown-eyed teenager named Cathy-from-Boston caught my attention on a ferry boat at Word of Life Island fifty-one years before.

14

A Companion for the Final Laps

New turf. Unfamiliar territory. It was like I had just stepped off a plane in a foreign land. I had been serving my wife and children for nearly five decades. It's all I knew. After the flurry of activities surrounding Cathy's death (like entertaining family and taking care of paperwork), I found myself living in a huge house *all by myself.* I honestly did not know how to handle myself. It was sterile Stonehaven, and it had Cathy's fingerprints on every wall and in every cabinet and drawer. The day after Cathy died, I had gone around the house and removed all the traces of Cathy's suffering and sickness so at least I didn't have to be reminded of the hard days. But all the good memories were still there. She had created a collage of photographs—perhaps two-hundred-fifty pictures—of our family memories, and it was all *glued* to the hallway wall. I had to pass it every time I walked into my study or the bedroom wing of the house. They were wonderful memories, but they represented the past, and the past was past. This was the present. How was I to live now?

I recalled the time twenty years earlier when my friend and ministry partner Randy Williams had invited me to go on a trout fishing trip with him and his dad on the Yuba River. He said they only had room for one more guy. So I joined them and had a great time of fellowship for a few days in the Sierras.

But the first day on the river was a time of surprising mental confusion for me. I would throw my line into the water and look around for my boys, thinking I needed to help them with their poles. But they weren't there. After a while I started feeling guilty for enjoying the experience because I wasn't doing anything for anyone else. You see, many years before I had quit bringing my own fishing pole when I took my kids out so I wouldn't be distracted from helping them. And now I was just fishing for myself, and it seemed incredibly selfish. Even though I knew my boys were all better fishermen than I was at that point, I still felt lost without serving them.

I felt the same way about cooking a meal for myself. Should I sit down ceremoniously and pretend like I'm sharing dinner with someone, or should I just stand by the counter and wolf down the food in survival mode? It honestly felt wrong to do either. One day shortly after Cathy died, I was shopping for supplies in the grocery store. Oroville's a small town, and you seldom go to the store without running into someone you know. I ran into a friend and did my customary, "Hi, how are you," and then started to move on. Suddenly I realized I was free to stand there and talk for twenty minutes if I wanted. I was not responsible to anyone at home—no kids, no loving wife, nobody. And I didn't know how to be around women. I had no idea what appropriate social boundaries I should be observing. This freedom was enslaving my mind.

Crying out to the Lord became my daily pattern: "Lord, I desperately need Your help learning to be a single man. Please show me the way ahead. I feel lost. You promised to complete the good work in me that You began when I committed my life to Jesus many years ago (Philippians 1:6). I'm counting on You."

Soon I sensed our tender Heavenly Father encouraging me to follow my old familiar path. I should seek counsel from people who had more experience with this than I did. So I took two steps. (1) I located a website which offered resources to widowers and read half a dozen books written by men who had lost their wives. I found myself connecting deeply with the painful emotion of their journeys. It was wonderfully cathartic. I realized my experience was not unique. And (2) in early November I reached out to five older singles I knew from church, one man and four women. I invited them to dinner at Stonehaven, and told them I was seeking their counsel on how they did life without a spouse. Over taco salad, I asked them each how long they had been single. It was a wide range from one year to forty-five years. Later, as we sat by the woodstove, I asked them to each give me their personal secrets of living the single life. I listened intently, and learned something helpful from each one. But I was particularly drawn to one of them who seemed the most comfortable in her singleness—she was the one who had been alone for forty-five years. And what she had to say really struck a chord on my heartstrings. She said she had learned to deepen her connection to Jesus whenever she felt the loneliness of missing a human partner. And she said something about cultivating human friendships at a level I knew nothing about. Her counsel intrigued me, and so I asked her if it was appropriate for me to meet with her for coffee to have her teach me more. And she was happy to help. She said she had male friends and female friends, and it was entirely OK for me to be seen with her in a coffee shop.

Thus began my life-transforming coffee chats with Dixie Gilbert, as we explored what we dubbed Miss Dixie's Friendship 101 class. Dixie had been part of my disciple-makers team, and she had helped us in our investment business. She had been a dear friend to Cathy, and had been one of her chauffeurs. And she was the one for whom I had built the wooden cross several years earlier. I think we had coffee once in December, once in January, and a couple times in February. At the end of 2017, I was busy traveling to see some of my kids over the holidays, and then when I returned I started putting together a men's discipleship group as well as attending a class called GriefShare to help me with the loss of my precious Cathy. I was also winding up the last project of my investment business, and I was showing my rehabbed house for sale. Within a few hours, I received two offers on the house. There were pros and cons with each offer, and I felt conflicted. It was a moment when I used to rely on my prayer partner, Cathy, but she wasn't there. I felt stymied. So I thought long and hard. What had Dixie been teaching me? Call your friends, even if they are females. So I called Dixie and asked her to pray for me. She did, and as soon as I hung up the phone, I knew which offer to accept. It was the right decision, and the deal went smoothly and quickly.

It was a cold Monday morning in early February 2018. I stood warming myself by the woodstove at Stonehaven looking out over the crystal clear winter view. I was taking stock of my life. I realized I was truly in a challenging, new, unfamiliar place, and in order for me to be able to fit into my new environment, I needed God to help me become a new man—no small order for a man in his seventies. I started thinking about the passage which had meant so much to me as I was ending my sabbatical fifteen years earlier. It reads, in part: "But we have this treasure in earthen vessels, so that the surpassing greatness of the power will be of God and not from ourselves" (2 Corinthians 4:7, NASB). The treasure is the presence of Jesus as He indwells these old cracked pots with

His powerful Holy Spirit. I knew I needed Him very badly. So, from the depths of my soul, I cried outloud to God, "Lord, I desperately need a complete new infusion of Your powerful treasure into this old earthen vessel." I felt the burden flow off my chest and onto the heart of my Father, and so I went about my business as usual for the rest of the day.

Since it was Monday, I had practice at 6:00 PM with my gospel bluegrass band with whom I'd been playing bass for several years. I loaded my bass into the car and drove to practice. I came walking into the venue carrying my bass, and our lead guitarist, Darrell Loomis, said to me, "Guess what I've been doing today? I've been writing a new tune to your song. Wanna hear it?"

So as I listened, I was amazed that God had given him such a fresh and up-tempo setting for the old hymn God had given me back in 2003. He went on to say, "The words are too good to lay buried. They needed a new suit of clothes."

Well, I was blessed, to say the least. But it wasn't until I got home that I realized the magnitude of what God had done for me that day. My old song was entitled, "This Earthen Vessel." Darrell had infused it with new life for a new era. It was a parable of my life. I had cried out to God in the morning, and at *the very moment I was praying,* He was stirring in Darrell to write the new tune. It was as if God was lifting my bowed head and infusing me with fresh hope! He was indeed going to make me into a new man for a new era. Thank you, Darrell, for being so sensitive to the Holy Spirit that day!

With the sale of that final investment house, I sat down and took stock of my financial affairs. The numbers added up. For the first time, I could actually retire. And the real estate market had completely changed in the eight years I had been doing investing. I could never have gotten into the market now. God had seemingly sent the discounted market just for me during the years I needed to build my retirement. Now it was over. I had set a goal eight years earlier, and by God's grace, I had been enabled to reach it.

The signposts were pointing to a serious turning point in my life. God knew he was preparing me for a wonderful new life with Dixie. But neither Dixie nor I knew it yet.

The first five months of 2018 became one of the most tumultuous and emotionally draining periods of our entire lives. Both of us were constantly gushing tears whether alone or together, our hearts regularly beating out of our chests. As we look back from this vantage point…it's obvious what was going on. God was breaking into our lives at a very deep level. Dixie was being a good friend in order to teach me how to be a good friend, and I was trying to learn from her lessons. Since she had told me the M-word (marriage) should not be part of our conversation, only friendship was on the table. But while trying to learn from her about being a friend, I was being drawn to her as an amazing friend and woman of God. I was still grieving the loss of Cathy, so it didn't seem right that I could or should be falling in love with Dixie. But I thought about her all the time. I mean *all the time*.

We longed for the times at the coffee shop together. But we knew it was just friendship. Both of us cried out to the Lord for help when we were apart, and we leaned on the counsel of trusted, spiritually-minded friends. Surprisingly, none of them encouraged us to end the friendship. Even they sensed that God might be doing something. We began to communicate by email. She would write me amazing words of spiritual nourishment from her laptop in bed late at night. I would read them and weep. Then I would meticulously craft my email responses, being extremely careful to not say anything that went beyond the boundaries of friendship. What was going on?

At one of our coffee sessions in early March, I made a suggestion. "Dixie, you have a cross out at your place. I have a great love for the Lord's Table. Would you consider inviting a few of our mutual friends to a "Communion at the Cross"? She accepted, and it was a wonderful experience! It gave us a sample of how our gifts and abilities worked in harmony, and it gave us a chance to pray together—something which immediately began to unite our hearts in a deeper way.

At this point we were thoroughly conflicted! We were delighting in our times together as friends—especially our times of prayer. And she was being extremely "friendly"—inviting me to lunch and coffee and over to her house for chats on the porch (often lasting for hours), cooking meals for my men's mentoring group, etc..... She insisted this was nothing more than deep friendship, but I was receiving romantic overtones, and it made me crazy!

There came a memorable day in early April when our relationship would have come to an end if God had not directly intervened. I was so confused by her seeming gestures of love which she maintained were mere friendship that I said, "I don't think I can do this, Dixie. I'm drawn to you, but I can't just be friends."

At that moment, God stopped me in my tracks as we were praying. He spoke quite clearly to me saying, "Ron, you can do this in My strength." I told Dixie what He had just said. She agreed that this was indeed a "special" friendship, and if God approved, it was worth pursuing.

Then, just a few days later, in her daily journaling God confirmed this to her by saying, "I have some wonderful things for you, Dixie, but you have to let Me give you Ron for this to happen." She began opening to the idea that God was doing something very special which might impact her singleness.

In the middle of April, Dixie flew to Mexico to be with her son John and his family as they were preparing to cross the Pacific to Hawaii in their forty-five foot sailboat. Those ten days of separation became a huge turning point in our love affair. Now it wasn't just me thinking about her all the time; she came to terms with the notion that she was also thinking about me all the time. (We have the voluminous emails to prove it.) When she returned, things began to move rapidly, and we allowed the word love to enter our dialog.

Frequent times of sharing prayer and communion (amid copious tears of joy) at the outdoor cross on her property became the milestones which defined our rapidly blooming love. A few days after she returned from Mexico, I prepared a communion meditation, and we formally presented our *friendship* to the Lord at the foot of the cross. Things moved so rapidly during the next few days, that within another week we were at the cross again having communion and, this time, presenting our *courtship* to the Lord. Our love was out in the open now, and every day was electric. The emails were flying at all hours of the day and night, and we were constantly and tearfully overwhelmed with the palpable presence of God.

Now this was weed-whacking season in Northern California (first week of May), and so on a warm Thursday afternoon I donned hood and ear muffs and plunged into the tall weeds at Stonehaven. Moments after I began, God suddenly began speaking audibly to me. It was what I would later describe as a "monumental download." He reminded me that fifteen years earlier, He had signaled the major transition from my life in Woodland as a pastor to my new life in Oroville by giving me a song. Then He declared, "Now you're entering a new season of your life, and I'm giving you another song. Only this time the Song is with a capital S, and she has arms and legs (which I later came to understand was contrasted with Cathy's cancer-weakened hands and feet), and she has a deep well of love for you."

He went on to tell me I was finished with my life of real estate investing, because, He said, "You're going to have your hands full with ministry and loving Dixie." Monumental indeed!

Needless to say, within two more days she accepted my proposal of marriage, and we were at the cross again with bread and wine, this time presenting our *engagement* to the Lord. It was May 5, a mere fourteen days from the *friendship* communion. We prayerfully set October 6 as the wedding day. We knew God wanted me to move to her place. So the toasty summer was spent undertaking the merger of our disparate lives. Dixie needed to be introduced to all my big family, and I needed to meet Dixie's son John and his family. (God graciously enabled these introductions to go exceedingly well.) We knew we must host the wedding at the cross because it was such an important piece of our story. I resigned my part-time position as Discipleship Pastor at our church. I built a two-hundred square foot study in one corner of her barn. And I began to pray about letting go of Stonehaven.

The wedding in October was a day to remember. My brother-in-law Duane Davidson performed the ceremony; and he wryly observed that both Dixie and I had obviously failed her Friendship 101 course! That's a class I'm glad I flunked!

I heard a story once about a man who dreamed about running the Boston marathon. So he trained long and hard, but when the day of the contest arrived, he wasn't able to complete the race because he ran out of strength in the last part of the journey. He was quite discouraged. So his friend, also a runner, decided to coach this man to run the marathon again the following year. He gave him tips on better training, and then made a plan to help the man finish this time. The friend positioned himself alongside the course near where the man had petered out the year before. When the man reached that fatal stage of the race, his friend suddenly emerged from the sidelines and started running alongside the man. He handed him a banana to replenish his energy and started chatting with the exhausted runner, speaking words of encouragement. The man found his second wind, and this time he was able to make it safely to the finish line because he was alongside his cheerleader-coach. That's how I feel about God's miraculous provision of Dixie. She was waiting single on the sidelines for forty-five years, and He sent her to join me in running these last laps of my life journey.

After our honeymoon, we began the daunting task of emptying Stonehaven and preparing it for sale. But God was with us every step of the way. There was a huge need for household items because thousands of people had been displaced by the fire which destroyed the entire city of Paradise, California. So I watched numerous truck and trailer loads of items leave my place to find new homes with displaced people. And then God enabled me to sell Stonehaven to a couple who themselves had lost their beautiful home in that devastating fire. The chapter on my old life was closed. The chapter on my new life was just beginning.

In fact, the changes in me were so conspicuous that my son-in-law, Bethany's husband Mark, started referring to me as Ron 2.0. And I felt like Ron 2.0. It was an emotionally wrenching transformation from 1.0 to 2.0, but it was accomplished by that same transforming grace which had been at work in my life since the earliest days. God knew what I needed, and His Spirit, that indwelling treasure, made it happen because He wasn't through with me yet.

An example of the radical makeover God has worked in me is my relationship to dogs. I mentioned earlier that the dog bite I suffered at age seven created a serious life-long dislike in me for canines. Yet while my heart was being united with Dixie's, God was also opening it to her dog Bo. In the midst of the emotionally turbulent times of our courtship, Bo adopted me as his new friend, and I found that sixty-plus-year-old wound of canine antipathy being healed.

However, an indispensable part of the old Ron 1.0 is still present with me, which is my love of the simplicity of the early church. In the spring of 2019, Dixie and I prayerfully sensed the Spirit leading us out of the traditional, building-based church into fellowship with the organic/house church/simple church. God is doing amazing things around the earth via small, simple expressions of Christ's body which meet in homes, and we have been drawn to them. Seldom does a week go by that we are not sharing prayer and scripture around a meal and the Lord's Table in our home with others who love the simplicity of just the essentials. We have felt like we have finally returned home to our roots.

I look around at other folks my age who have gone through painful trials. Many of them are just plain bitter and grumpy and depressed about life. They could be investing their life experience and wisdom in younger people, but they've given up. For a variety of reasons, they're not allowing their Redeemer to adapt them to their new circumstances. I look at myself today, and I realize it's not like that for me! I have hope and the prospects for continued impact in the lives of many people even though I'm in my seventies. God has given me a partner who amplifies and facilitates my giftedness, and although I may be less energetic at seventy-three than I was back the the days of Ron 1.0, I'm still investing what I have for the kingdom.

Years ago when I was in the throes of ministry in Woodland, I had an encounter with God which left a permanent mark on me. I had just returned from the wonderful summer trip with my family. We'd been gone for three months. Before I left, I had met with several people who had enthusiastically pledged to take on various aspects of the ministry while I was gone for the summer. Some of them were promising to organize certain aspects of the building remodeling project. So when I returned, I began checking in with the various people to get reports on their efforts for the summer. Many—if not most—of the promises had not been kept. One particular brother had been exceptionally vociferous about his enthusiasm just before I left. But when I returned he had turned vitriolic. He hadn't done what he promised, he said, because he realized he had great disdain for me and the ministry of Woodland Bible Church. He compared us to things you flush down the toilet. He, like many others, had a key to the building. He stood there red-faced across a table telling me his reasons for leaving. Then he quite theatrically grabbed his key from his pocket, slammed it on the table, and shouted, "That's the last you'll ever see of me." And he stormed out.

It felt like a gut punch. I slowly wandered out into the dark auditorium. I mean *dark*, because there were no lights, and the skating rink ceiling was painted black. This brother's outburst was like the straw that broke the camel's back. I had been absorbing various blows of criticism ever since I returned from my trip, and I was done. I screamed at the top of my lungs, "God, I quit. If that's how I get treated for giving my best, it's not worth serving You."

And then the room was eerily silent. The darkness spoke volumes. And then I heard the voice of God say, "Ron, why are you quitting? I haven't given up on *you* yet."

Slowly the tears started to well up and I got on my knees and confessed my weakness. I remembered Elijah trying to quit. God didn't give up on him either. So I had a time of renewal of my promise to serve Him if He would use this weak old earthen vessel.

And He did. That moment when I almost gave up was a turning point in my years in Woodland. Issues that plagued us constantly during the early years started to be resolved, and the ministry started prospering more and more. Times of major crisis are the times when God shows some of His most amazing miracles. My recent transformation into Ron 2.0 with Dixie at my side is the sweet fruit which my Lord has wrought out of the crucible of my pain after the loss of Cathy.

My story is a lot like the book of Acts. It is officially known as "The Acts of the Apostles," but it is more properly named "The Acts of the Holy Spirit Working Through a Bunch of Ordinary People Who Had the Courage to Live by Faith." As I said earlier, I titled this book "Lines in Pleasant Places" because I feel l have received a gracious inheritance from my Heavenly Father. The title comes from Psalm 16:6: "The [boundary] lines have fallen to me in pleasant places; indeed, my heritage is beautiful to me" (NASB). One's inheritance is a gift from the parents, and it is often reflective of the relationship which the parent feels towards the heir. And such it is with our life with God. My glorious inheritance has included all the early experiences God allowed in my life which trained me and exposed and healed ugly weaknesses in me. It has included all the moments where He spoke power into my life when I felt nothing but weakness. It has included mountains of undeserved gifts and blessings. It has included a measure of fruitfulness for His kingdom—lives whom He has touched through me. It has included a family of precious, amazingly bright and talented children. And it has been crowned with two incomparable women as partners whom I never deserved. In fact, I don't deserve *any* of my rich inheritance. How sweet is His amazing grace that saved a wretch like me! It's because of His grace that my heritage truly is beautiful to me.

My sweet daughter said it quite eloquently at Dixie's wedding shower a couple days before our wedding. She was talking about her dad, and she said, "It's amazing to me that my *dad*, the nerdy geek, has been blessed with two such amazing women for his wives!" I say a hearty "Amen!"

One of my purposes in composing this book is to heap glory on my Creator and Redeemer! When He created me—like He does with all His creatures—He instilled great deposits of potential in me. Sin did a serious job of tainting and damaging what God created in me—just like it has done in every person He has created. However, praise God, in His superabundant grace, He has shown me the broken places and has forgiven and is healing them with His redeeming blood. Redemption means the damaged potential is restored so it can shine again as the Creator originally intended. I've told my stories to encourge you that you are not left to fight your way out of your brokenness alone. Because He loves us, the Redeemer specializes in reclaiming and transforming our dormant potential energy into powerful kinetic energy all for His glory! Our Creator and Redeemer does magnificent work! I pray that the stories of my life are exhuberant testimony to the way He has poured Himself into this old earthen vessel, exhibiting Himself as the living, loving, miracle-working, prayer-answering God!

Too often, I believe, Christianity is wrongly seen simply as a religion which people choose because it suits their liking and makes them feel good. But I pray that my life is a testimony to the premise that following Jesus is the only rational response to the reality that He came back from the dead after being brutally killed to atone for our sins, and that He is truly alive and active today in the world, both transforming people and working miracles in the lives of those who love Him. I challenged Him to manifest Himself to me in a dorm room in Longview, Texas, in 1965, and as I write these words, there is no doubt in my mind He has answered my challenge. I know He would answer you if you would also similarly challenge Him.

Made in the USA
San Bernardino, CA
25 June 2020